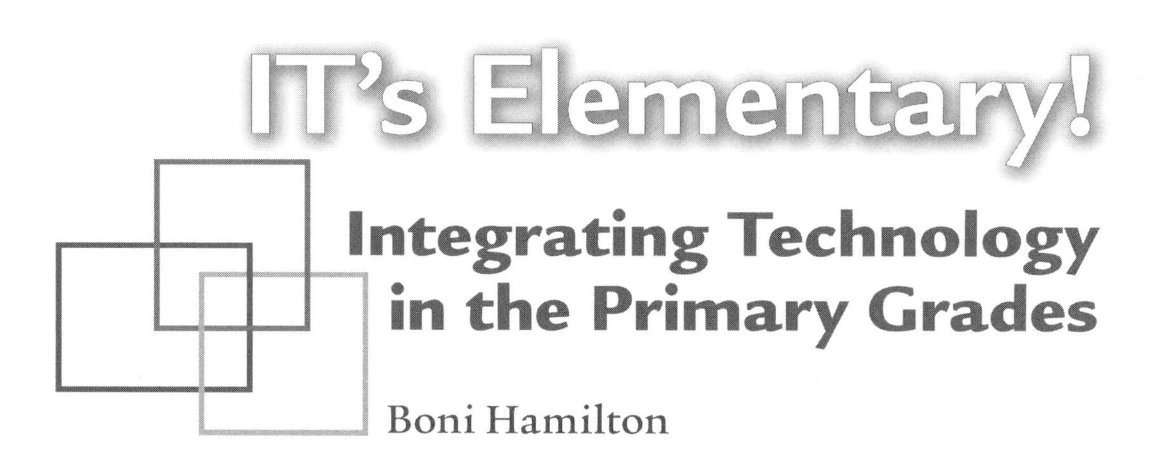

IT's Elementary!

Integrating Technology in the Primary Grades

Boni Hamilton

International Society for Technology in Education
EUGENE, OREGON ▪ WASHINGTON, DC

IT's Elementary!
Integrating Technology in the Primary Grades

Boni Hamilton

ACQUISITIONS AND DEVELOPMENT EDITOR
Scott Harter

PRODUCTION EDITOR
Lynda Gansel

PRODUCTION COORDINATOR
Maddelyn High

GRAPHIC DESIGNER
Signe Landin

RIGHTS AND PERMISSIONS ADMINISTRATOR
Diane Durrett

COPY EDITOR
Mary Snyder

COVER DESIGN
Signe Landin

BOOK DESIGN AND PRODUCTION
Lina Van Brunt and Rakar West
Van Brunt/West Design

International Society for Technology in Education (ISTE)
Washington, DC, Office:
1710 Rhode Island Ave. NW, Suite 900, Washington, DC 20036

Eugene, Oregon, Office:
175 West Broadway, Suite 300, Eugene, OR 97401-3003

Order Desk: 1.800.336.5191
Order Fax: 1.541.302.3778
Customer Service: orders@iste.org
Book Publishing: books@iste.org
Rights and Permissions: permissions@iste.org
Web site: www.iste.org

First Edition
ISBN: 978-1-56484-228-2

About ISTE

The International Society for Technology in Education (ISTE) is a nonprofit professional organization with a worldwide membership of leaders in education technology. We are dedicated to promoting appropriate uses of technology to support and improve learning, teaching, and administration in PK–12 and teacher education. As part of that mission, ISTE provides high-quality and timely information, services, and materials, such as this book.

ISTE Book Publishing works with experienced educators to develop and produce practical resources for classroom teachers, teacher educators, and technology leaders. Every manuscript we select for publication is carefully peer-reviewed and professionally edited. We look for content that emphasizes the effective use of technology where it can make a difference—increasing the productivity of teachers and administrators; helping students with unique learning styles, abilities, or backgrounds; collecting and using data for decision making at the school and district level; and creating dynamic, project-based learning environments that engage 21st-century learners. We value your feedback on this book and other ISTE products. E-mail us at **books@iste.org**.

ISTE is home of the National Educational Technology Standards (NETS) Project, the National Educational Computing Conference (NECC), and the National Center for Preparing Tomorrow's Teachers to Use Technology (NCPT³). To find out more about these and other ISTE initiatives and to view our complete book list or request a print catalog, visit our Web site at **www.iste.org**. You'll find information about:

- ISTE, our mission, and our members
- Membership opportunities and services
- Online communities and special interest groups (SIGs)
- Professional development services
- Research and evaluation services
- Educator resources
- ISTE's National Technology Standards for Students, Teachers, and Administrators
- *Learning & Leading with Technology* magazine
- *Journal of Research on Technology in Education*

About the Author

Boni Hamilton has been writing and teaching for more than 25 years. She has taught all ages, from preschoolers to adults, and in a variety of contexts, from regular K–12 classrooms to special education, gifted/talented, and ESL classrooms. Boni began using computers in 1975 when her husband, John, bought a TRS-80 with his first student loan. She received a BA in English from Bethel College (MN) and an MA in Educational Leadership from the University of Northern Colorado. Currently, Boni is Assistant Director for Instructional Technology for Littleton Public Schools in Littleton, Colorado. She and John have two adult children, Nick and Jamie.

Contents

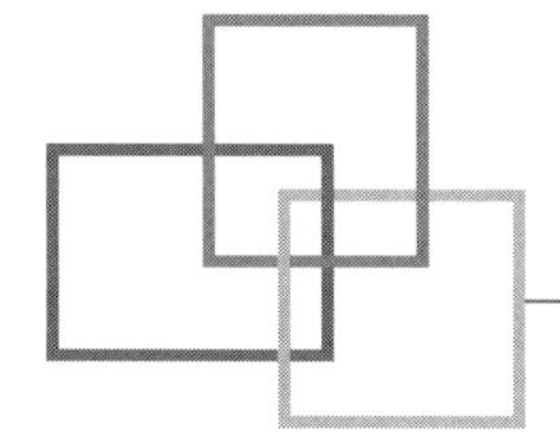

Introduction

Technology Integration at Lois Lenski Elementary School

IN APRIL 2004, A SITE COMMITTEE OF LIBRARY SPECIALISTS representing the American Association of School Librarians (AASL) conducted a two-day site visit at Lois Lenski Elementary, near Denver, Colorado. The specialists observed classes, looked at student portfolios, and interviewed students, teachers, community members, and district staff.

Their goal: To assess Lenski's library media/technology program for evidence that, by working in collaboration to plan, teach, and assess students, the library media staff and teachers were implementing a cohesive instructional plan to train students to access and use information effectively.

By the end of the visit, the specialists commented not only on the seamless integration of library skills with content area instruction, but how uniquely Lenski had blended a strong technology program into the partnership of classroom teachers and library media specialists to enrich students' experiences. On the recommendation of the site visit committee, Lenski was named the elementary school winner of the 2004 AASL Library Media Program of the Year.

I'm part of the Instructional Technology team for the Littleton Public School District, which includes Lois Lensky Elementary, and that site visit from representatives of AASL changed my perspective about the role of technology in a school. Until then, I had defined Lenski's model as a triangle where classroom teachers, the library staff and the technology teachers collaborated on what were essentially separate programs. The synergy of several individuals with complementary skills talking regularly about students and their academic needs resulted in better instruction in each setting: the classroom, the library, and the computer lab.

During the site visit by AASL, I saw that Lenski's model had moved beyond that original model. The library and technology programs overlapped with classroom instruction to provide seamless instruction. The placement of computers in both the library and classrooms offered students opportunities to continue their computer work in either place. The use of online databases for gathering information meant that research could happen in the classroom and computer lab as well as in the library. And the close collaboration among the classroom teachers, library media specialist and technology teacher made everyone responsible for student success.

Even more important, the library and computer lab had become true extensions of the classroom. Teachers referred to them as "additional learning spaces" rather than as special locations for different learning experiences. The same learning objectives guiding classroom instruction permeated the activities and instruction in the library and computer lab. Students heard consistent vocabulary, worked toward the same goals, and faced uniform expectations for content area mastery. The only difference: Students had access to additional instructional experts in the library and computer lab to assist with their use of technology resources.

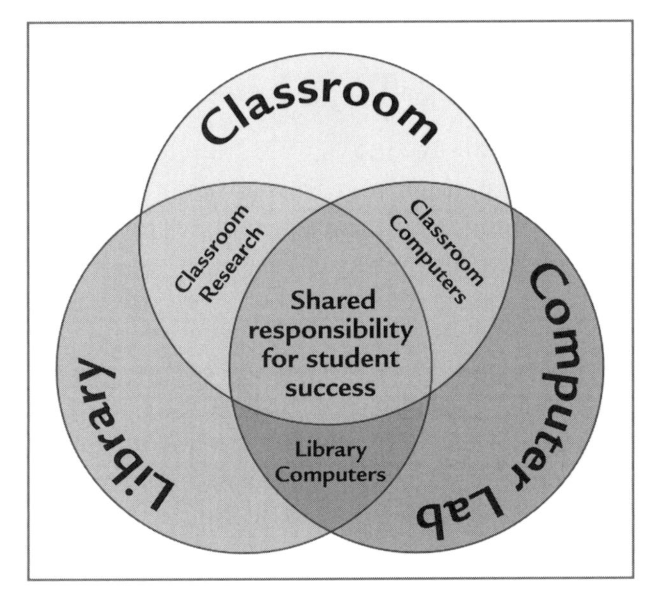

FIGURE 0.1 This graphic represents Lenski's current integration model. The collaboration among the classroom teachers, librarian, and technology teacher has blended the three learning spaces so that the responsibility for student success has become a shared task.

Technology in Action

Eight to ten visitor groups tour Lenski weekly, often without advance notice to the school, so guests see classes going about their normal business, not pre-planned agendas. Invariably, visitors comment on the role technology plays in supporting students' mastery of curricular content.

An example of a typical visit would be when Dr. Shirley Trees, Director of Elementary Education for Littleton Public School District, brought three elementary principals to conduct a walk-through of several classes at Lenski. The walk-through focused on student engagement and on-task behavior.

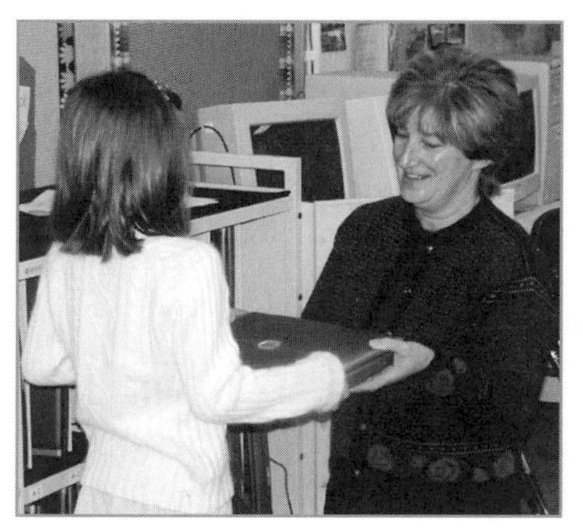

FIGURE 0.2 Second-grade teacher Gerri Morahan kneels to hand a wireless laptop to one of her students. Even though Gerri herself is a computer novice, she gives her students many opportunities to use the wireless laptops and classroom computers. By the end of the year, her students have developed great problem-solving skills.

The group started at the computer lab where a first-grade teacher explained that she and a technology teacher had collaborated on a unit about nutrition. In the classroom and during the past two computer lab sessions, students used books, Web sites, and outside experts to learn about food. As a culminating activity, students drew pictures of nutritious foods and added three-clue riddles to the drawings.

In a second-grade class across the hall, students using wireless laptops worked in desktop publishing software to create books about the inventions they'd made. Based on an earlier literacy lesson about the format of nonfiction books, the students were adding tables of content to their books. The classroom teacher and a parent volunteer supervised, although much of the computer assistance came from peers.

Students in a fifth-grade class clustered around classroom computers to work in teams on the Bill of Rights. Using presentation software, student groups were creating slide shows, with one slide per amendment. They were required not only to bullet the major points of each amendment, but also to illustrate the ideas by combining clip art, call-outs, and drawings.

The principals ended their walk-through in a fourth-grade classroom where students also worked in teams. Each team of four had been assigned a Native American tribe from a region of the United States. They were writing group essays on the tribe's culture, creating group slide shows, and individually authoring folktales based on their tribe's belief system.

In each classroom, students took little notice of visitors until directly approached with a question. Then they eagerly showed off their work and explained the purpose of the tasks. During the debrief session, the visiting principals commented on students' focused attention to their work. They speculated that the use of technology increased the level of engagement in the classrooms. And, because students drew upon the curricular content to complete their projects, they could explain the connection between what they were doing and what they had learned.

Visitors typically see a lot of technology in action when they observe classes at Lenski, and each year the infusion of technology into classroom learning increases. As teachers improve their use of technology to deliver and assess knowledge, they create more powerful learning opportunities for students. For Lenski teachers, the use of technology is no longer an extra; it truly is a natural part of their teaching repertoire.

School Profile

Lois Lenski Elementary School is a K–5 school with about 600 students in the Denver suburb of Centennial, Colorado. One of 15 elementary schools in the Littleton Public School District, Lenski is currently the newest and largest. Lenski's attendance area covers seven neighborhoods, but because Colorado endorses school choice, almost half of the students optionally enroll from outside the attendance area.

FIGURE 0.3 Lois Lenski Elementary School is nestled in a suburban neighborhood south of Denver. Part of the Littleton Public School District, Lenski has slightly more than 600 students, fifty percent of whom are optionally enrolled.

Lenski has four classes at each grade level, with an average class size of 25. Approximately 20 percent of Lenski students are identified as gifted/talented, and a similar percentage qualify for special education services. In addition to special classes in art, music, and physical education, Lenski students can take a variety of before- and after-school enrichment classes in visual art, instrumental music, performing arts, foreign language, academic interests, and technology. The percentage of students who qualify for free or reduced lunch is lower than 10%. Parents volunteer thousands of hours and raise significant support dollars for the school.

As would be expected from a high socioeconomic school, Lenski students perform well on state and national assessments, and the school is annually rated Excellent by the Colorado Department of Education. In 1999–2000, Lenski was named a Blue Ribbon School of Excellence by the U.S. Department of Education.

However, some statistics about Lenski's performance cannot be explained away by socioeconomic status. Except on the state's third-grade writing assessment, Lenski does not show a gender gap in reading, writing, or math. This contrasts with many schools where girls outperform boys in reading and writing while boys outperform girls in math. Most interestingly, this gender gap was closed at Lenski without the teachers consciously working to equalize performance.

The staff believes that technology provides gender-neutralizing effects. Word processing seems to help boys be more effective in evaluating their writing and making improvements, particularly when they use the text-to-table process described in chapter 8. Students improve their reading comprehension when they read and respond to large amounts of text during the research process. Because that research is often done in cooperative groups, students also help one another interpret what they read, which provides more immediate feedback to struggling students than a teacher can often manage. Then too, students work cooperatively to turn what they've learned into products that convey the essential concepts—another skill that builds reading and writing skills.

The use of virtual manipulatives in math gives students instant feedback, so they and their teachers recognize when students need to revisit a concept. Also, computers can be used in ways that differentiate for learning preferences as well as for ability level. Students who learn best when they interact with other people (generally girls) can cluster their computers and coach one another. Students who learn best when they are interacting solely with a computer or teacher (generally boys) have that option with virtual manipulatives and other math software and Web sites.

At fourth and fifth grades, where state and district scores show a 15–20+ percentile gap between state reading and writing assessments, Lenski students show less than a 10-point gap. The Lenski gap has been closing steadily for several years as Lenski students improve in their writing achievement. Teachers observe that the use of technology to improve student writing results in better writing even when students are not using technology. Making a distinction between editing and revising as well as using the tools of text-to-table to help students see where they need to improve (as described in chapter 8) helps students become conscious of bad writing habits and good writing practices.

While separating the effects of technology on achievement from the effects of other good instructional practices (such as cooperative learning, reciprocal teaching, role-playing, and visualizing) may be difficult, if not impossible, watching students enthusiastically tackle projects that entwine technology use with demonstrations of curricular learning leaves no doubt that the use of technology engages students in higher-level thinking about what they've learned.

The Evolution of Lenski's Technology Program

The Lenski community has valued technology since the school received its first computer in 1984. All classrooms shared that one computer. Veteran teachers remember learning the new terminology: keyboard, mouse, and monitor.

At first, no one knew how to use computers in schools, and teachers everywhere welcomed the advent of educational software. By the early 90s, Lenski had created a computer lab stocked with a variety of educational software programs. From the beginning, Lenski administrators understood that unless classroom teachers accompanied their students to the lab, no one would integrate technology with classroom content.

In 1999, I accepted a position as Lenski's new technology teacher. I inherited a program where classroom teachers attended lab with their students and attempted to integrate the lab lessons with classroom instruction. Lenski's technology program was considered one of the strongest in the state, even though the lab held only 15 computers for classes of 25 or more students, and classrooms typically had only one computer that was Internet-ready. Many teachers valued technology and liked being involved in planning lab lessons for students. The lack of computers frustrated them because it limited what their students could accomplish. A few teachers seemed intimidated by technology. They typically depended on specialty software that allowed two students to share a computer for drill exercises on basic skills.

Because I volunteered at the school during the 1998–99 school year, I had shadowed the technology teacher twice a week for several months prior to becoming the computer teacher myself. I quickly realized that I didn't know enough about computer troubleshooting, curriculum, or specialty software. My ten years as a high school English teacher in the late 70s and early 80s predated the use of computers in schools, and I had learned my computer skills in the business world. My knowledge about teaching elementary students came from volunteering while my children attended Lenski.

I approached Lenski's technology program with several beliefs:

- **Students learn best when they are controlling the mouse themselves.** Lenski's practice of having students share computers would not work for me as a teacher. Too often the student with no mouse to handle eventually tunes out. I want every student involved every minute of the lab. To accomplish this, I would need to acquire more computers for the school so that every student would have a computer to control during lab. This belief also had implications for my teaching—if I believe students should control the mouse for themselves, I needed either to ask their permission to use the mouse when I helped them or to teach them how to solve problems themselves.

- **Any computer is better than no computer.** In my experience, children adapt to technology far more easily than adults. In practice, this meant I could solicit donated computers without a concern for what platform they were—the students and I would learn to be competent on both PC and Mac platforms.

  In 2000, Lenski had 37 two-year old Macintosh G3s with one in each classroom for the teacher and 15 in the lab. Classrooms generally had one or two Mac Classics and/or Apple IIes, which had been acquired in the late 80s. In addition, in a little-used hallway, a lab of 27 Apple IIes served primary teachers for additional drill software. The students had access to two black-and-white printers, one temperamental ink jet color printer, one ten-year-old scanner, and two digital cameras. The fourth- and fifth-grade teachers valiantly tried to share the classroom computers so that students could work on projects outside the lab, but they experienced constant frustration, not only with the lack of equipment but also with equipment that constantly failed. Teachers identified reliability as their highest priority for classroom equipment.

  When I launched a donation program to provide additional equipment for classrooms, I accepted that the computers would be several years old. However, given that equipment in schools often stays in use more than ten years, even a three-year-old computer likely would have more power and speed than the equipment currently in the classroom.

- **Students could accomplish as much with basic office software as with specialty software.** Donated computers will not necessarily run specialty software, and the school lacks the money to upgrade. Because of my business background, I believe that office productivity software has more relevancy anyway, so I focus on finding appropriate ways to use word processing and presentation software, in particular.

- **Teachers need to feel safe acknowledging what they do not know.** To take the pressure off teachers, I advocate placing a lab computer at an angle so that no one but the computer teacher can see it. Classroom teachers can use this computer when they need to practice the same skill that the students are learning.

  Providing this kind of safety net for teachers pays off quickly. Teachers model learning for students, without students necessarily knowing the mistakes the teachers make. Within a short time, though, most teachers realize that, rather than criticizing those who don't know a skill, students love to coach. This empowers teachers to take risks with technology in the classroom as well, because they trust that the students can help one another.

- **Effective staff development in technology is differentiated and individual.** When I plan technology staff development, I usually offer at least three choices based on teachers' requests. Most of the time, though, I use a "skills-as-needed" model. Teachers remember more when they have authentic reasons for learning, so any time a teacher needs to know a skill, I give individual training. Because of a grant allocation, teachers have laptops for their daily use. Now teachers can ask for help at home as well, which relieves the technology staff from providing as much skills training as in the past.

- **Teachers should decide how many computers they want in their classrooms.** We acknowledge that all classrooms differ, so one teacher may need only two computers while another needs fifteen. That's fine. I'd rather a teacher chose to have one computer and use it to support student learning than impose a higher number that never get turned on. Because the school pays licensing fees based on how many computers are in the school, teachers are thoughtful about how many they request. However, teachers can have as many computers as they will use regularly in their classrooms.
- **Technology is integrated into curriculum, not taught as a stand-alone or parallel subject.** I teach technology skills when students need them in order to produce content-driven projects. The classroom teachers determine the projects and the content. This collaboration between the classroom teachers and the technology teacher leads to richer experiences for students.
- **We have a responsibility to share our best practices with others.** The factors that make Lenski fortunate—supportive principal, collaborative staff, eager students, and involved community members—also place obligations on our shoulders. Every year, Lenski teachers join me in presenting aspects of our technology program to visitors and at conferences. We also initiate relationships with other schools by offering training and/or equipment.

Lenski's Technology Staff

Lenski has always placed high value on having technology support for teachers and the lab. Because the school has more than 600 students, and every class in grades 1–5 spends at least one hour a week in the lab, Lenski needs at least one full-time teacher to teach in the lab.

But the technology needs in a school like Lenski extend beyond the lab. Equipment fails, students accidentally change computer settings, teachers ask for one-on-one training, printers get jammed, secretaries request help creating reports for parent communications, the Web site needs to be updated, the cafeteria manager runs into a glitch right before the lunch rush, and the Information Technology Services (ITS) department asks for inventory reports or software upgrades. Just the challenge of maintaining 300 computers could keep a full-time technician busy! Additionally, the technology teacher serves on the leadership team and may be asked to take visitors on tours, attend district trainings, or handle a disciplinary problem.

So, Lenski always has at least two people, and sometimes three, whose primary responsibilities involve technology. How Lenski configures the help depends on the level of funding and availability of staff each year.

FIGURE 0.4 Since 1999, Lenski's technology support team has included (left to right) my husband John Hamilton, my first teaching partner Marj McDonald, the current technology teacher Trecie Warner, and me.

In my first two years, I partnered in the technology program with Marj McDonald, who had been a third-grade teacher. We made a great team because we were so similar in vision, risk-taking, and dedication. When Marj left Lenski to become an administrator, I paired up with Trecie Warner, who is now Lenski's lead technology teacher.

In fact, Trecie joined Lenski staff during my second year and worked as a flexible support person for the school before she took Marj's place. This enabled her to get familiar with Lenski's staff, philosophy and culture before she started to co-teach with regular teachers.

As Trecie grew more comfortable with handling the lab, I took more responsibilities for leadership in the school. I tried to balance my teaching load with handling district reports, troubleshooting equipment, and supporting all staff, including the district library staff housed at Lenski.

In 2005–06, the superintendent plucked me from Lenski to work on district strategic planning for the growth of instructional technology at all schools. While I negotiated a portion of my contract to support Lenski, my primary responsibilities at the district prevented me from teaching students and providing leadership at Lenski.

Trecie took on the responsibilities for teaching in the computer lab, solving equipment problems, and providing staff development for technology. Even with two teaching assistants, Dana Wilhelm and Suzette Bowles, to support her, Trecie struggled to juggle the demands of a large school. The teaching load alone requires a minimum of 22 hours out of 27.5 instructional hours per week! Even though those classes are co-taught by classroom teachers, Trecie needs to present the technical skills and to assist students. If her job only involved teaching, Trecie could stay busy every day, but she also needs to troubleshoot and maintain five wireless carts, six color printers, and countless other technology equipment being used in classrooms while she is in the lab.

In 2006–07, while I continue my district position, Trecie will not only have Dana and Suzette as assistants, but will also turn some lab classes over to a former classroom teacher.

For some schools, this level of technology support may seem excessive. But Lenski places a high value on the use of technology to support student learning, so the technology team carries a heavy instructional and support burden. Without several people involved in the technology program, Lenski teachers would not continue to move forward.

As the scope of technology integration increases at Lenski, so do the demands on the technology team. Managing the network and 300 computers requires more time than Lenski's team has. While other schools might use the district's ITS personnel for support, Lenski has made decisions that have placed the responsibility of almost all technical support on the school rather than the district. Enter our most supportive volunteer—my husband John.

Despite John's full-time job as an engineer in a medical device company, he gives no less than 15 hours a week, and often more, to Lenski to support the technology program. From the beginning, he and I developed Team Tech, a cadre of volunteers who spend one evening a week refurbishing and repairing computers. Lenski's technology infrastructure came out of John's head and was shaped by his fingers. Despite his extensive knowledge of technology, he constantly researches to learn more. Truthfully, many of the changes at Lenski were made easier by John's expertise and his relationships with teachers. Every school should be blessed with a volunteer like John!

For schools that lack the volunteer support that John and the Team Tech give, and that can't staff a technology program as fully as Lenski does, integrating technology with curricular content is still viable. Schools with strong support from the ITS department won't need the level of volunteer commitment that Lenski uses. Many schools receive daily or weekly district technical support for equipment and network maintenance.

If the district also provides creative and enthusiastic specialists to work with teachers on integrating technology, then some of the school-based staff may not be necessary. In smaller schools, the technology teacher might have more flexibility to support classrooms as well.

Finally, as teachers grow more comfortable and competent with integrating technology, they can depend on one another for ideas and assistance rather than always counting on the technology teacher. Lenski teachers have been developing their own ideas for several years, but they still value the perspective a technology teacher gives in terms of organizing a project or developing a template.

Pacing the Change

In my six years at Lenski, my technology partners and I have probably attempted too much too quickly. We are lucky the classroom teachers didn't revolt. The changes introduced over the past six years should have been spread over eight to ten years. Somehow the momentum created by a few small changes, such as more computers for students and laptops for teachers, built into an irresistible force. In my first two years, Lenski teachers migrated from Macs to PCs; adapted their instruction to include digital cameras, scanners, LCD projectors, and wireless mobile labs; and significantly increased their personal use of computers.

Even more important, the teachers began designing sophisticated, content-driven projects rather than depending on specialty software. Prior to the changes I made in the program, some teachers had regularly used skill-practice software. With this software, students wore headphones and, quite frankly, teachers often took a break from instruction. I resisted using this software because teachers had to adapt their lessons to the software rather than the software adapting to what students needed to practice.

As I have worked with teachers to develop projects that support their units of study and to locate Web resources to allow students to practice basic content skills, teachers enjoy the power to adapt work in the computer lab to match their classroom instruction. This represents a major shift in thinking among the staff.

Teachers have summer opportunities to attend technology conferences, and they often return to Lenski with new ideas for old equipment and software applications. They also propose the acquisition of new equipment. What excellent revenge for the years when I pushed them out of their comfort levels! Often the new ideas they propose prod me into new territory. We have learned as a staff to consider each proposal through the lens of instruction. Will the idea or equipment improve instruction? Will students be pushed to higher levels of thinking or achievement? Is it a gimmick that will be abandoned when the novelty wears off? Is this the next appropriate step?

At Lenski, where all staff have opportunities to participate in decisions, making technology-based decisions as a group fits the school culture. A Curriculum Innovation Team (as proposed by Plan for Social Excellence, www.pfse.org, for its Technology Grant) of teachers oversees the implementation of the technology program at Lenski. Originally, I expected this group to rubber-stamp my recommendations, but from the first decision, the CIT has demonstrated independence.

The CIT represents teachers' best thinking about technology needs in the building. Sometimes they address teachers' staff development needs; other times they consider the equipment needs of the building. The CIT suggested that new equipment be placed first in the lab and library so that all teachers can see it demonstrated before it appears in the classrooms. This gives teachers a sense of how the equipment will improve their instruction and primes them to *want* to adopt it.

When we have not demonstrated new equipment, such as the AlphaSmarts and student digital cameras, in the library and lab first, teachers have delayed adopting the changes.

The following lists the order of major equipment purchases at Lenski based on CIT decisions. Almost all new equipment has been bought through grants.

1. Projector and interactive whiteboard for the lab
2. Four color printers
3. Ten digital cameras and twelve scanners
4. Laptops for teachers and support staff
5. Four LCD projectors, one for the library and three on carts for classrooms
6. Mobile carts of laptops for student use (3 carts of 15 laptops)
7. AlphaSmart portable word processors for classrooms (6 per room)
8. Two more mobile carts of laptops, one primarily for library use
9. Eight sturdy digital cameras for student use
10. One document camera for the library
11. Document cameras and LCD projectors for every classroom

Each roll-out of equipment has energized teachers to rethink how they use technology with their students. Sharing these ideas has recently become the thrust of staff development for Lenski teachers.

Lenski's Progress

As mentioned earlier, when I started at Lenski, some of the greatest challenges that many schools face today had already been addressed. For instance, Lenski had always considered the use of technology in instruction a teacher's responsibility, so the computer lab was not part of a special rotation. Also, Lenski's administrators understood the necessity of placing strong instructional leaders in the library and computer lab. They convinced the community that the benefit of these professional support staff would offset slightly larger class sizes. Lenski also already had a strong collaborative model. In fact, when I started, Lenski had just been named a Blue Ribbon School of Excellence by the U. S. Department of Education.

As an already successful school, Lenski had no motivation to embrace transformative change. Yet, the culture of the staff is to continually seek improvement in instruction and student achievement. When I started in 1999, some teachers believed that they could use technology more effectively and had started to explore the power of the Internet and productivity software. My knowledge of advanced technical skills, good instructional practices, and sources for inexpensive technology tools made us excellent partners.

Providing additional computers became the first priority. I wrote to 20 local mid-sized companies to request any working computers that they no longer needed and could donate to a school. Three companies responded immediately. One offered ten complete, plug-and-go systems while the other two offered a mix of parts. From those donations, with the volunteer help of high school students and community techies, we refurbished enough equipment in the first year to fill the lab with 30 Internet-ready Macintosh computers, replace Apple LCIIs in classrooms with donated PCs, restock a mini-lab with 10 PCs, place 6 PCs in the library, and create a second lab of 28 PCs for math practice software.

While the volunteer program worked on equipment the first two years, Marj McDonald and I focused on helping teachers design meaningful technology-based projects that would reinforce, extend, enrich, and assess student learning. Because we were still developing our philosophy of effective integration, we experienced as much frustration and failure as we did success.

The previous technology staff had carefully documented the projects and lessons they used at each grade level. This was a rich resource, but because all students now had their own computers in the lab, lessons took half the time they had in the past. That meant we needed to come up with at least as many new lessons as we already had. Additionally, because computers were now available in classrooms, the library, and the mini-lab, students often completed projects during class time. Lessons that had been planned to cover three weeks suddenly became one-lab lessons.

Marj's experience as a third-grade teacher gave her the advantage of recognizing the capabilities of elementary students and knowing the curriculum. I was often clueless, so I depended on teachers to help me. In fact, Lenski teachers began to use curriculum mapping primarily to show me the flow and timing of curricular units.

Not all teachers embraced the changes in that first year. Some continued to prefer specialty software and headphones. For me, the regular use of specialty software provided a chance to evaluate its instructional value as compared to project-based learning. Since I had experience only with Lenski's computer lab model, I needed a year to evaluate a range of instructional practices and develop a philosophy of effective technology integration. Regular conversations about instruction with Marj, librarian Marcia Parrish, and principal Barb DeSpain helped shape my vision.

Today, Lenski teachers have almost completely abandoned using specialty software because of its lack of flexibility. If software requires a teacher to adapt instruction to it rather than the software adapting itself to students' needs, then Lenski teachers agree that the software isn't appropriate for content-area instruction.

In the process of applying for grant money to fund the volunteer refurbishing program, I stumbled across Plan for Social Excellence (PFSE), a foundation with a Technology Grant replication program. PFSE funded a three-year grant for Lenski that permitted the school to purchase equipment, including laptops for all teachers,

FIGURE 0.5 Lenski teachers Tina Kelly and Sue Holt work together on laptops during staff development training. The laptops gave teachers the flexibility to work at home and resulted in a sudden improvement in teachers' technical proficiency.

and pay for staff development. The laptops gave teachers the flexibility to work at home and resulted in a sudden improvement in teachers' technical proficiency.

Because classroom teachers co-teach in the lab, they have many opportunities to learn new skills, particularly teachers at the intermediate grade levels. The rest of the staff worried about falling behind. Out of the necessity of addressing so many needs, I presented highly differentiated staff development. In addition to providing two or three choices during staff development meetings, the technology team also offers one-on-one, just-in-time training. However, eventually teachers' access to laptops diminished their needs for individual training because they could tap other people outside the school, such as their friends and family members, to help them.

Lessons learned over time include:

1. Good integration of technology with content knowledge changes instruction. When students use technology as a tool to express what they know, the focus moves naturally from teaching to learning. The most effective teachers release students to discover information, work collaboratively, and take responsibility for demonstrating understanding. They encourage students to apply their new knowledge to solve real problems or to form opinions.
2. Technology simplifies differentiation. Projects can easily be modified at either end of the spectrum without the modification being obvious to students. Also, because many struggling students experience greater success with technology than with traditional tools, they can produce projects with a high-quality look even if the content is modified. Interactive Web sites also address the needs of experiential and visual learners better than many classroom activities. Students who need supplemental practice on skills often prefer computerized practice to other forms.
3. Everyone changes eventually, even resistors, but the degree of change differs. Not every Lenski teacher whole heartedly embraces technology to support instruction. In fact, some persistently resist. In some cases, teachers think technology detracts from, rather than enhances, instruction. In others, the resistance reflects a personal unease with technology and/or management of the classroom. In my experience, resistors typically teach the way they were taught; they

have not shifted their instruction from focusing on what they teach to what students learn. The battle is much larger than just technology integration. However, compared to their attitudes during my first year, resistant teachers are using technology more often and more willingly today.

4. The more tools you put in the hands of students and teachers, the more technology becomes a natural and personal expression of their thinking. Personal laptops empower teachers to improve their own skills, including changing their computers to reflect their working styles. Wireless laptops and portable word processors in classrooms enable students to work, individually or cooperatively, to create products that demonstrate what they have learned and improves their higher-level thinking skills. When students take cheap digital cameras on field trips, they choose to photograph different scenes from the ones their teachers typically select. Teachers take pictures of students learning; students take close-ups of what they are learning about.
5. The use of a teacher-only committee to control decisions about technology leads to effective change. Any staff member who is interested may attend Lenski's CIT meetings and participate in decisions. Those who are involved in the decisions then have an advocacy responsibility to help other teachers embrace the change.

Recently, Lenski's teachers shared their best ideas with a visiting principal. During the sharing, teachers awaiting their turns listened with rapt attention to the projects being done at other grades, projects they could imagine adapting to fit their grade-level content. Later, the teachers proposed to CIT the idea of twice-monthly optional meetings where teachers can highlight projects that their students have completed. The optional sharing suggestion has generated excitement among teachers because they believe it will make them more effective users of technology to support students' academic progress.

Lenski does not try to stay at the cutting edge of technology use. For one thing, Colorado's per pupil funding ranks near the bottom of fifty states, so Colorado schools have little money to spare for technology purchases. What new equipment the school acquires almost always comes from grant money or parent fund-raising.

The staff also stays conscious of instructional responsibility. Some new technology tools fit so closely with instruction that adoption comes quickly. Consider document cameras. As soon as teachers saw the document cameras in use in the library, they could list a number of ways to use the cameras to improve instruction. In fact, when the document cameras were delivered to the school, teachers unboxed them and put them into action without waiting for inventory tags or technical help.

However, until the document cameras had been introduced, most teachers did not consider the LCD projectors necessary for the classroom, even though the teachers regularly saw the projectors in use in the library and computer lab. The few projectors on mobile carts ended up almost permanently housed in the few classrooms where teachers saw their potential to change the dynamics of instruction. Now that Lenski teachers need projectors to take advantage of their document cameras and the district's license for streaming video, the LCD projectors have become valued tools to the same teachers who a year ago considered projectors superfluous.

The final issue in the deliberate choice not to be on the cutting edge is the wide variety of tools available. Years ago, a former principal at Lenski was listening to parents discuss the PTO programs at other district schools that Lenski PTO did not offer. He cautioned them that they needed to base their decisions about PTO programs on the needs of Lenski students and not on the "grass is greener" concept. Lenski staff keeps that guideline in mind. No one can or should use every tool and adopt every great idea in technology. Sometimes great technology tools simply do not fit the style or needs of a particular school. Lenski has transformed instruction through the use of the technology tools that fit the school. The pace and process of that change has been deliberate. Some ideas and tools have been deliberately ignored—not because of deficiencies in those technologies, but because we choose to do what meets our students' needs.

The purpose of this book is to encourage and empower change at other schools, not to replicate Lenski's program. All schools have unique needs and opportunities. The common trait should be the use of technology as a transparent support for preparing students to thrive in the 21st century.

PART 1

Strategies for Planning and Implementing a Technology Makeover in Your School

Chapter 1

The Philosophy of Integration

AFTER MORE THAN TWENTY YEARS OF COMPUTERS IN SCHOOLS, technology integration in education should be ubiquitous and no one should need to write a book about it. After all, technology has infiltrated all aspects of our daily life, and we rarely even notice it. Yet, teachers still talk about "doing a technology lesson" as though teaching with technology is somehow different from "real" teaching. After all this time, the process of integrating technology with content area instruction remains a mystery to many teachers.

Why Integrate?

I believe that *the integration of technology with classroom content improves student achievement.* Thoughtfully planned, such lessons engage students to a higher degree than traditional teaching and lead to the development of 21st-century skills such as complex thinking, creative problem solving, and collaboration.

Not everyone agrees that technology integration improves student learning. Some argue that research results have been mixed, and they are correct. Yet, overall, the evidence seems to support the belief that appropriate use of technology results in higher student achievement and involvement.

Creating a definitive research study to measure the effectiveness of technology integration has serious challenges. First, technology includes many devices beyond the computer: digital cameras, the Internet, student information systems, multimedia devices, LCD projectors, and a plethora of other tools. Then too the tools may be used in multiple ways: programmed learning, skills in isolation, project-based learning, simulations, tutorials, multimedia presentations, video conferencing, etc. Narrowing the scope of a research study to only one technology tool and one technique eliminates the central component of integration—the infusion of many forms of technology into content-area instruction to meet the diverse needs of students.

The evidence that convinced me about the effectiveness of technology integration was data analysis at Lenski. When I looked at data concerning students' academic growth, based on state, national, and school-based assessments, I found that students' academic growth was significantly higher in classes where teachers used technology widely. Other factors such as teacher skill, student mix, and parental participation may have also influenced achievement in these classes, but students cited the frequent use of technology as a motivator in their classes.

Lenski's data also contrasted sharply to surrounding schools on the issue of gender differences. While many schools scrambled to address significant gender gaps in reading, writing, and math, Lenski consistently showed no gender gaps in any of those areas over six years except for a couple of years in third-grade writing. Third-grade boys lagged behind girls in writing performance on state tests, but made up the gap by the fourth-grade tests. Lenski staff believes that the use of technology mitigates gender differences.

What is Integration?

To clarify what the term integration means, one must first understand what it does NOT mean. Integration is NOT the use of managed instructional software, where a computer delivers content and tracks students' progress. Integration is NOT having students go to a computer lab to learn technical skills while the classroom teacher stays behind to plan or grade papers. Integration is NOT using the Internet to access games sponsored by toy manufacturers or popular television shows. Integration is NOT using specialty software for drill and practice day after day. Integration does NOT replace a teacher with a computer.

Integration is when classroom teachers use technology to introduce, reinforce, extend, enrich, assess, and remediate student mastery of curricular targets.

Integration is an *instructional choice* that generally includes collaboration and deliberate planning—and *always* requires a classroom teacher's participation. It cannot be legislated through curriculum guides nor will it happen spontaneously. Someone with vision—an administrator, a teacher, or a specialist—needs to model, encourage,

Research on the Effectiveness of Technology Integration

In 1996, Stratham and Torell reviewed 10 meta-analyses on how technology impacts student learning. They found that computer technology, when implemented properly, could profoundly impact student learning.

They reported the following findings:

- Student performance on tests: "When properly implemented, the use of computer technology in education has a significant positive effect on student achievement as measured by test scores across subject areas and with all levels of students." (Stratham & Torell, 1996.)
- Impact on classroom instruction: "When used appropriately, computer technology in classrooms stimulates increased teacher/student interaction, and encourages cooperative learning, collaboration, problem-solving, and student inquiries." (Stratham & Torell, 1996.)

Both of these findings indicate how important it is for teachers to be thoughtful about the implementation of technology use in the classroom. The second finding also highlights how appropriate use of technology in a classroom can change teaching practices.

- Impact on student behavior: "Students from computer-rich classrooms show better behavior, lower school absentee rates, lower drop-out rates, earn more college scholarships, and attend college in greater numbers than do students from non-computer classrooms." (Stratham & Torell, 1996.)

This finding seems to support increasing students' access to computers in the classrooms. At Lenski, a computer-to-student ratio of 1:2.5 allowed teachers and students to accomplish their work without frustration, even though some of those computers in the ratio were reserved for adult-only uses such as the library check-out system and administrator computers.

- Impact of computer use on subgroups: "Computer-based teaching is especially effective among populations of at-risk students." (Stratham & Torell, 1996.)

At-risk students not only have barriers to their learning, but they often struggle with confidence as well. At Lenski, at-risk students build confidence as they master computer skills and coach classmates.

For those who need more repetition of basic skills than their classmates, we often can find Web-based practice drills that they can use at home or during free time at school. Drills don't seem onerous when students are setting their own pace and interacting with a computer.

A literature review by James A. Kulik in 2003 compared meta-analyses of research prior to and after 1990. He concluded that, although the research was at times contradictory, overall, instructional technology is growing increasingly effective at the elementary and secondary levels (Kulik, 2003). This finding seems to acknowledge that over the past decade teachers have had access to more equipment, Internet-based resources, and lesson ideas than in the early years of computer use.

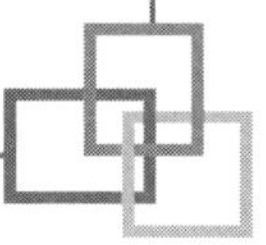

and enable integration, but only a classroom teacher can integrate technology with content-area teaching.

Can a classroom teacher integrate technology without collaboration? Definitely! Some teachers infuse technology into their classroom instruction without involving anyone else. Whether their students use technology in the classroom, a lab, or the library, the teacher takes full responsibility for planning, monitoring, and assessing the lessons. However, the likelihood of consistent, persistent, and purposeful integration increases dramatically when classroom teachers include others in their instructional plans.

FIGURE 1.1 First-grade teacher Diane Vyhnalek is always looking for new ways to engage her students in discovery and higher-level thinking. Here she uses a document camera and projector to look closely at dragonflies in different stages of the life cycle.

Can a computer teacher, even a master teacher, integrate technology with classroom content without the involvement of a classroom teacher? **No!** Not even if the computer teacher knows the curriculum better than the classroom teacher. No one but the classroom teacher has the knowledge of where the students are in their mastery of a concept and what curricular targets need reinforcement or assessment. Every class is different with different needs.

Even though all four first-grade classes at Lenski study insects, how the teachers use technology to support the unit differs widely from one another and from year to year. One teacher combines insect study with independent research. Students read about insects and write simple reports. On the computers, they illustrate their reports with drawings of the insects. Another class focuses on recognizing insect body parts. They visit Web sites where they can practice identifying insect body parts and culminate their unit with detailed, labeled insect drawings generated on the computer. Another teacher focuses on habitats, so her students' labeled drawings include the insects' habitats. The fourth teacher combines insect study with observation, questioning, and inferential thinking. Using a Web site with hundreds of photos of dragonflies, she and the students link what they see in the photos to what they've read about dragonflies. They engage in rich conversations about all aspects of dragonflies' lives, including speculating about why some wings have missing pieces and why different species of dragonflies have different coloration. During this dragonfly study, the students scramble to find information that will answer their questions until they are experts on dragonflies. They then apply what they've learned about one insect to the general category of insects.

The computer teacher can address curriculum through technology, teach rich lessons on curricular units, deliver instruction that helps students meet state or national standards, and affect students' academic progress overall. But, without the involvement of the classroom teacher, the lessons in a computer lab are supplemental, not integrated.

The classroom teacher provides the link between the technology project and classroom learning. Prior to lab sessions, the classroom teacher identifies where students are in their mastery of curricular targets and suggests areas where students need reinforcement. This knowledge drives the design of lessons.

The classroom teacher also ties technology lessons to classroom experiences through examples, references to classroom conversations, or pre-instruction. The teacher clarifies vocabulary, expectations for finished products, and timelines. Without the involvement of the classroom teacher, computer lessons stand alone.

Many computer teachers and paraprofessionals teach stand-alone lessons that tie into curricular objectives. Their lessons are well conceived and expertly taught. This *parallel teaching* supplements classroom instruction because it reinforces essential knowledge and, at the same time, teaches essential skills for a technology-based future. While parallel teaching supports students academically, it doesn't link as tightly to their classroom learning as a lesson conceived by and co-taught by the classroom teacher.

In thousands of other computer labs though, the lessons have no connection to curricular content. In this model of *isolated teaching,* computer teachers simply create projects that use the computer skills they believe students should know or send students to game sites with little educational tie-in. Often, these isolated lessons are simply play times for children.

If, when teachers are using technology to support content-area instruction, they also follow best instructional practices for improving student achievement, their students are highly likely to become better readers, writers, mathematicians, scientists, and thinkers.

Consider how the use of technology connected to content-area instruction can incorporate the nine instructional strategies that have a positive effect on student learning (Marzano, Pickering, & Pollock, 2001):

- Identifying similarities and differences. At any grade level, teachers can use technology to help children compare and contrast, classify, or link information. While Venn diagrams probably come to mind first, students can identify similarities and differences though other computer tasks. They can draw pictures that illustrate similarities and differences in content-area units such as seasons, insect body parts, and planets. Writing similes and metaphors requires students to make connections between two unlike things. Students can even draw illustrations of analogies within poems or work on Web sites where they separate words by initial sounds.

- **Summarizing and note taking.** When students glean essential information from what they read or hear, they improve their recall of the information. Creating a slide show presentation requires students to distill their information into a few bullet points that will convey their messages. Students can also take two-column notes in a spreadsheet or word processing application.
- **Reinforcing effort and providing recognition.** Students do not always understand that effort pays off. When they set reading goals and then graph the results after a trimester, they can take pride in their accomplishments. Studying famous people who made a difference in the world will highlight for students the connection between effort and recognition. At any grade level, students can create portfolios of their work—periodically looking back at where they started and what they've accomplished can motivate students to continue working hard.
- **Homework and practice.** Homework is most effective when students do it without parental involvement. By third grade, students can practice keyboarding independently at home. If students have Internet access, they can use a number of free Web-based keyboarding resources listed in chapter 7. Teachers can also recommend Web-based drill activities to help students master basic skills.
- **Nonlinguistic representations.** Vocabulary words stick when students use drawings as well as definitions. Check out the Dictionary Day and Idiom activities in chapter 9 as good examples of nonlinguistic representation. Even before they can read and write, primary students can express their understanding of curricular targets through pictures. Graphing provides another way for students to understand relationships in numbers.
- **Cooperative learning.** Students in computer-rich classrooms are more likely to use cooperative learning (Stratham & Torell, 1996) to complete their work. Teachers can promote cooperative learning through assigning teams to complete short projects, such as writing dialogue in pairs, or longer assignments, such as researching an aspect of space exploration.
- **Setting objectives and providing feedback.** Having students create their own questions for research projects encourages them to set the objectives for their study. They then can focus on the aspect of curriculum that piques their interest. The use of virtual manipulatives gives students instant feedback on math concepts, as do many other Web sites that engage students in basic skills practice.
- **Generating and testing hypotheses**. Students can predict what will happen when they gather data for graphs, virtually build and test machines online, and solve logic problems on Web sites. Young students can place pictures in sequential order, complete a pattern, or match pictures of bird beaks with food sources.

- **Questions, cues, and advance organizers.** When questions, organizers and other tools are used prior to instruction in a curricular unit, the tools help students identify what is important to remember. Teachers can introduce a unit through wordless slide shows. With a pictures-only slide show, students draw conclusions about the unit from the pictures they see. This also gives them visual anchors for the text they read. Introducing primary source photos and audio clips at the beginning of a unit on immigration or state history, for instance, can help students generate the questions they want to research.

A teacher who can combine these nine strategies that have a positive effect on student learning with curricular content supported by the use of technology will develop rich learning experiences for students and improve achievement.

Requirements for Integration

To successfully integrate, schools must have the following resources:

Administrative Support. The role of the administrator cannot be overstated. The integration of technology and library skills (information literacy) must become a non-negotiable within a school or the technology program will never change. Making such a change in a school is not easy and probably cannot be done quickly. A truly supportive administrator ensures that:

1. *Classroom teachers understand the responsibility for planning and teaching content-based technology lessons.* Schools use different models for delivering technology support. In some schools, classroom teachers accompany their students to a lab and co-teach the lesson with a technology teacher. Other schools have eliminated labs and expect all technology use to happen within the classroom. One school, which treats computer lab as part of the specials rotation, changed its delivery model so that classroom teachers pre-teach the technology lesson in the classroom and the technology aide assists students when they work in the lab.
2. *The school is staffed with professional library and technology staff.* If a district already provides the funds to hire professionals in these roles, then those schools have an advantage. However, in many schools, the library and technology positions are filled with teacher assistants, who, despite their excellent intentions, often do not have the knowledge base or staff development opportunities to become instructional leaders. Professionals in these areas can model lesson design, collaboration, and instruction.

   Lenski has opted to increase class size slightly and use the extra staffing dollars to pay for full-time professional support in the library and lab. The district's average class size is 25, but, at Lenski, 25 is the minimum, with a maximum of 29 students. The community and staff know that the support from the professional library and technology staff helps teachers during important instructional times.

3. *Computer teachers are treated as colleagues with professional status, regular planning time, and staff development opportunities.* Asking teachers to co-plan and co-teach with classified staff often backfires because of the difference in training and status. Computer teachers need to attend the same staff development as the classroom staff. Then they can use the same instructional methods and language as classroom teachers so that students hear consistent messages. Additionally, administrators should consider placing their strongest instructional models in the library and computer lab. In a strong library/technology program, these two support teachers model instruction for all students and all classroom teachers. In fact, because of their regular work with all students, the library/tech staff may actually be better at diagnosing when an intervention to address barriers to achievement is needed.
4. *Professional growth plans for classroom teachers include goals related to technology integration.* Initially, teachers should submit at least one lesson plan for a technology-based unit and completed student samples to the principal annually. Eventually, though, technology integration should happen so regularly that such goals can be dropped from the professional growth plan.
5. *All staff receives ample opportunities to learn best practices in technology integration.* This may be the hardest task, in fact, because of a glut of poor models and dearth of excellent models. However, most schools and school districts can identify a few staff members who integrate technology in some aspect of instruction. These teachers can be tapped to either present staff development or host observations in their classrooms. If the school has the capability to videotape teachers using best practices in technology integration, the videos can be used as resources.
6. *Teachers feel safe taking risks.* Integrating technology requires changing how staff members interact, plan, and instruct. Teachers must feel safe and supported while they experiment with change. This may be as simple as allowing a teacher to abandon an idea that doesn't work out or as complex as redesigning the schedule to allow for collaborative planning time.

Staff Buy-in. Some schools ask teachers to manage all the technology use alone. Others, like Lenski, provide support staff to manage the computers, co-teach in a lab, conduct staff development in technology skills, and ease the load of planning technology units. Whatever the school's approach, teachers do not have to be experts in technology in order to integrate it. Often students' technical skills surpass the staff's, and students can coach one another. However, teachers do need to believe that the use of technology will help students reach curricular targets.

The effectiveness of a technology-based unit depends on a teacher's planning. Students' use of computers must be productive, which means it must enhance or reinforce content learning. That may require teachers to observe models of good integration so that they understand how to plan for and use technology. When teachers involve colleagues in their planning, the synergy of collaboration will result in even stronger instructional units.

Time and Tools for Collaboration. Many teachers are accustomed to closing their doors and teaching in isolation. They may plan major units with grade-level peers, but they have little experience co-planning and co-teaching a lesson or unit. Adjusting to team-teaching with the librarian and/or technology teacher may take time. This book offers tools and suggestions for initiating collaboration.

In addition, schools must provide time for collaborative planning. The pioneers, those who embrace change and take risks without fear, will make time, but other teachers may have to be prodded. Administrators can play a critical role by providing time, support, and incentives for collaborative planning. One technique that jump-started a school's program was a small grant that paid grade-level teams to meet one day during the summer with the library and technology staff. They planned major units and talked about possible ways to integrate information literacy skills.

Equipment. Most schools place their emphasis here, but it is the least important resource. Certainly, integration is easier when a teacher has a wealth of technology equipment—imagine the possibilities with a class set of wireless laptops in every room!—but a committed teacher can integrate technology even if only one Internet-ready computer with the basic office software suite is available. Lessons in an equipment-poor environment may not have the same scope, and a teacher may face daunting obstacles, but even in this environment, appropriate use of technology can impact student learning. This book will provide suggestions for how to adapt in an equipment-poor environment and how to acquire equipment.

Where to Start

Some schools don't currently have the necessary resources to fully integrate technology with classroom content. Rather than giving up in despair, individuals in schools should start the process of making changes in their areas and invite others to join. No matter what level of influence a person has in a school, everyone can take small steps toward making technology integral to instruction. A small spark may be all a school needs to get the engines going!

Administrators

Administrators who are frustrated by a lack of funds, equipment, teacher buy-in, or even technical support can focus on just one change that will make a difference for the school. Repurposing even a small amount in the budget for a technology purchase can energize a teacher to try a new technique. Perhaps a benefactor can supply a critical piece of equipment or the technology committee can pursue a grant. Hiring a technology integration pioneer for the next classroom opening can provide a model for other teachers. If teachers are required to add technology integration goals to their professional growth plans, they will have an impetus to try something new, especially if the administrator makes it clear that teachers are safe to take risks.

One strategy that has set several schools in motion has been the implementation of a teacher-only technology committee empowered with a budget. When teachers understand the vision for integration and are given money to spend for technology that will move the school ahead, they are motivated to increase their use of technology. The budget doesn't need to be large, but teachers do need the power to make the decisions without being vetoed by an administrator.

Administrators can also encourage teachers by sharing ideas for lessons, gleaned from this book or from an Internet search. One principal sends a new idea monthly to her staff to keep them thinking about how to integrate technology more effectively.

Computer Teachers/Coaches

Computer teachers depend on classroom teachers for collaboration. If computer lab is a drop-off special, lab lessons will be examples of parallel teaching. A lab teacher can recruit an approachable classroom teacher to at least co-plan a lesson. It may require the computer teacher to put out 75% of the effort, but once the students have completed a few curriculum-based lessons related to content, other teachers will be curious about how they can help the computer teacher design lessons that support the curriculum for their students. Over time, computer lab teachers can encourage teachers to be more involved in the lab planning.

Three good projects that parallel classroom content may be all a computer teacher can accomplish in a year. However, a project used with one class can generally be adapted to other classes and grade levels so each idea has the potential for lessons in multiple classes.

Classroom Teachers

Classroom teachers who lack either the support or time for technology integration can sift through the second half of this book for lesson ideas. For instance, since non-linguistic representation builds students' success in recalling information, a classroom teacher can ask students to use pictures to represent content-area vocabulary. Students will enjoy using the classroom computer(s) to create their illustrations. Displaying their work will improve all students' mastery of the vocabulary. Such a project works for any grade level.

Teachers will experience more success if they limit themselves to simple projects at first and a maximum of three new ideas a year. Each year they can build on the previous year's successes.

I've written this book to convey hope to readers. The integration of technology with classroom content instruction is a journey, not a race. Every step a school takes toward integrating technology more thoughtfully and purposefully will improve instruction for students.

Chapter 2

How to Get Started

WHEN COMPUTERS WERE NEW TO SCHOOLS, people had to invent ways to use them. Now that computers are present everywhere in society, the challenge for schools is finding the most appropriate and effective ways to use them. Unless the teacher connects the use of technology to content learning and effective instructional practice, students' time on computers is essentially a different form of recess. Students will not remember skills taught in isolation and do not learn higher-level thinking skills through most specialty software.

The most persistent question presented at our workshops is this: How can I get my school to change how we use technology in instruction?

The District's ITS Department's Role in the Change Process

If your district provides strong support to schools through the Information Technology Services (ITS) department, then this group can be a catalyst for change. ITS departments have two roles: technical/equipment support and instructional support.

On the technical side, ITS provides equipment and technical assistance to keep the equipment running. Some school districts replenish computers and other equipment on a three- or four-year cycle so that schools always have new equipment. In districts with the funding and a regular computer replacement plan, the access to new, reliable, and fast computers should enable schools to focus on the integration of technology with classroom content without the need to pursue outside grants and donated equipment. Lenski's dependence on the generosity of foundations and local businesses often drained energy and time from the technology and library staff that could have been spent nurturing teachers.

In my experience, the ability of ITS to provide adequate equipment depends on the per-pupil spending in a state or the ability of a district to tap local money for additional support. In Colorado, where per-pupil funding ranks near the bottom of all states and where schools have limited power to tap local funds, districts have little discretionary money for equipment. At Lenski, the district has provided fewer than 30 computers in six years.

Many school districts also provide regular technical support to repair and manage the technology equipment in schools. Take advantage of this if it's available. Having someone to solve equipment failures, train teachers on how equipment works, and repair poorly functioning computers frees the in-house staff to focus on people and content rather than machines.

On the instructional side, districts often hire specialists to help teachers plan for and execute technology-embedded units. Not all integration specialists are equal though. Administrators and teachers need clear explanations of how the specialists define their roles within the school, because the expectations vary from district to district and specialist to specialist. Some specialists narrowly define their roles as planners; they will talk with a teacher about a unit, but the teacher has all the responsibility to articulate the learning goal, generate the product ideas, choose the technology tools, and manage the unit. Some specialists see themselves as mentors. They model lessons or provide resources for teachers to use. In my opinion, the best specialists act as partners. They contribute ideas for lessons, model instruction in a teacher's classroom, and work alongside teachers to ensure success.

Depending on a specialist's workload, the partner model may take too much time for specialists to interact effectively with every teacher. At the elementary level, a specialist can work with a grade-level team to model how to collaborate on lesson planning, introduce a technology-infused unit, and assess students' progress. In schools where teachers have few or no role models working with technology, a good district specialist can spur the teachers to try new ideas and inspire confidence in the hesitant.

A potential resource outside the ITS department would be the district's staff developer. Moving teachers from technology in isolation to integration requires not just familiarity with technology, but changed teaching practices. If the school has access to a district trainer who can address constructivist teaching, differentiation, effective instructional practices, and project-based learning, then teachers will have a solid foundation on which to build units with technology as an integral part.

In any district where ITS offers strong customer service, schools should develop close ties with the best within that department. Using district resources as often as possible frees school resources—time and money—for implementation of new instructional strategies.

The Administrator's Role in the Change Process

Administrators have the greatest opportunity to speed up change because they control the building budget, the allocation of staff, and the vision. When administrators make a commitment to changing the role of technology in a school, staff members either buy in or bail out. This does not imply that the change is easy, just that a willing administrator can have a huge impact on how technology is viewed and used in the school.

The biggest hurdle most principals face is discontinuing the use of the computer lab in the specials rotation. As long as teachers send their students to the computer lab for someone else to teach, technology cannot be integrated into content learning. Only the classroom teacher can integrate technology because s/he determines the pace, depth, and purpose for instruction. The teacher determines whether to use technology to reinforce, extend, or assess student learning. And only the classroom teacher can take a project from the classroom to the lab and back to the classroom.

All student computers, whether in a lab, library, classroom, or on a wireless cart, become the classroom teacher's tools for instruction. Thus, a teacher's input is necessary for students to use computers effectively. Changing teachers' perceptions about the importance of their involvement with students in a computer lab or library takes time. Teachers need to capture the vision of how collaboration with the librarian and technology teacher increases and enriches instructional time and support for students. Time in the lab and library can be used as prime instructional times with classroom teachers directing the lessons according to their students' needs, while the librarian and technology teacher provide instruction on specific skills and assist struggling students.

Hiring professionals for the library and computer lab may strain the staffing budget, particularly if schools have been cutting library and lab services in order to achieve small class sizes. The two philosophies, small classes versus professional support in key instructional roles, often compete for the same dollars. An administrator needs to engage staff and the community in multiple conversations before making a change of this magnitude.

If possible, an administrator should choose strong instructional leaders for the library and technology positions. That way, all classroom teachers and all students have opportunities to learn from master teachers. The librarian and technology teacher can model best instructional practices for staff and can identify students or teachers who are struggling so that the administrator can offer support.

Principals are often hindered by their lack of expertise in integrating technology. They feel powerless to model integration, so they hesitate to demand integration from their teachers. No one needs to apologize for not knowing how to integrate. After six years of working with teachers to encourage and facilitate integration, I'm convinced that the transition from being a computer user to being a technology integrator requires more than intuition. In my experience, teachers need technical support, preliminary ideas for projects or lessons, and permission to try and, on occasion, fail. Once they begin to take risks with technology, each success will motivate them to try another idea.

Administrators can spur teachers to take risks by providing targeted staff development through conferences, classes, mentorships, or book studies. Beware staff development that actually retards change. Teaching skills in isolation doesn't work any better for teachers than for students. Every skills class needs to be attached to a purpose for using the skills. When teachers attend conferences, they should articulate their purposes for going, such as skill development, gathering ideas for projects, or canvassing the new products available for those that make a difference. After the conferences, administrators need to hold the teachers accountable to share what they've learned and to implement new ideas immediately. Most of the time, the software developer-sponsored workshops focus on selling software, not integrating it with your curriculum, so bypass these.

Incentives work for helping teachers change practices. The most effective incentive I've seen is giving teachers laptops. The expense might be higher than desktops, but the portability of a laptop enables teachers to work anytime at any place. When the gift of a laptop is tied to professional development, many teachers will participate with enthusiasm. Other incentives include paying stipends for time spent in learning new skills, covering the costs of classes or conferences, or offering in-service credit for in-house staff development. For some teachers, just the opportunity to take two half-days to visit other schools or classrooms where technology is well integrated may be incentive enough to try something new. At least two Lenski teachers are motivated by the promise that they can have an hour of staff development time to showcase their students' work.

When teachers try new ideas and persist to an end product, they need opportunities to share their students' work with the staff. Administrators should think about how to celebrate small successes to encourage others to make their own changes. Last year, several Lenski teachers spent more than an hour before school on a Friday in late May sharing their best ideas with a visiting principal. The time was so valued that the

Administrators' Approaches to Change

Several principals of my acquaintance are in the process of changing their elementary schools' technology programs. They each approach change differently, according to the culture and needs of their schools.

Principal 1

Three years ago, this school had a small lab of 15 computers as part of the library and very few computers in the classrooms. Traditionally, teachers sent half their students to the lab at a time while they worked with the remaining students in the classroom. Students learned skills in isolation and used little, if any, technology in the classroom.

The principal repurposed a classroom to be a lab and recruited enough donated computers to put 30 computers in the room. She set the expectation that classroom teachers would accompany their students to the lab and be involved in the planning and instruction. She also provided project ideas during grade-level collaborative time and, on occasion, modeled lab lessons.

The principal then purchased a class set of AlphaSmart portable word processors. She introduced them to the teachers by having the computer teacher take them to every classroom for mini-lessons on how to use them. Once teachers were hooked on how word processors could help them, the principal collected another round of donated network-ready computers to place in classrooms. After three years, the principal estimates that 60% or more of the staff are actively involved in lab lessons and most of those have also begun using technology regularly in their classrooms.

Principal 2

In the second school, the principal set a slower, more deliberate pace for implementing change. First, she gathered a technology committee of staff and community to develop a long-range plan for technology in the school. The committee contacted neighboring districts to learn about their technology leaders and visited each school. The committee also explored multiple models of integration to zero in on their own dream. Renovations to the school provided an opportunity to rearrange the floor plan, and the committee decided to dedicate one room for a computer lab and staff it with a teacher.

As soon as the lab was paid for, the principal began to set aside money to fill classrooms with technology tools. She will start next year with an LCD projector in every intermediate classroom and is pursuing the means to fit the remaining rooms with the same equipment. Meanwhile, teachers are learning through watching the computer lab teacher model how to use technology to support learning.

Principal 3

In this school, the principal could not alter the schedule to remove computer lab from the specials rotation. She decided that teachers would still be responsible for planning how students would use technology to support what they were learning in the classroom. She

continued

scheduled the computer aide to go into each classroom weekly to observe while the teacher explained to students the projects they would be working on during lab time. The aide then became a facilitator, not the instructor. The principal used a district focus on student engagement as the foundation for expecting teachers to increase their use of technology to support classroom work. Placing the expectations for technology lessons on the teachers raised their commitment to technology use and led to teachers using technology more effectively in their classrooms as part of daily instruction.

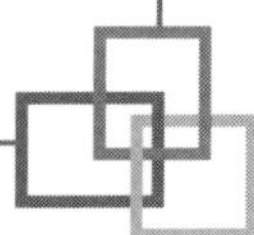

teachers have decided to schedule time for sharing every two weeks before school all next year. They will earn one in-service credit for the time, but more important, they will learn from one another.

The Technology Teacher's/Coach's Role in the Change Process

Some schools have disassembled computer labs to spread the computers to classrooms. In these schools, all technology use happens in the classrooms with or without technical support. If the school has technical support, the person may be a technician who repairs machines instead of an instructional support person. Teachers in those schools can partner with colleagues to brainstorm ideas and support one another.

The majority of elementary schools continue to support computer labs and personnel to run the labs. In fact, in a large number of elementary schools, computer lab is still in the specials rotation. At many of these schools, the lab supervisor is a teaching assistant, rather than a teacher.

The role of the person in the lab depends, first of all, on that person's status in the school. When the technology person is a teaching assistant, some staff members may balk at working collaboratively, no matter how skilled the computer person is. That happened to me when, during my first year, some teachers thought I was a volunteer mom turned staff. Even though they watched me teach in the lab and saw that I had expertise in both teaching and technology, a few teachers resisted collaborating with me. When word got around late in my first year that I not only had my teaching license, but also ten years of experience, I saw first-hand the change in those teachers' attitudes.

On the other hand, the majority of teachers welcome teaching partners, whether the partners have teaching degrees or not. Computer teachers should start working with the classroom teachers most willing to collaborate and let the momentum of successful projects sweep the other teachers in.

In schools that depend on labs, the computer lab teacher can often influence how classroom teachers build the confidence to take responsibility for using technology in the classroom. First, a computer teacher needs to know the curriculum for each grade level. That way, the computer teacher can suggest projects or Web resources that will support the content area instruction.

Next, the computer teacher can build a partnership with the librarian so that they can work as a team with classroom teachers to plan units. Projects that combine curricular targets, library research, and technology products provide high quality opportunities for students to understand the inter-relation of disciplines and learning spaces.

If teachers resist being involved with technology, and this is more common than it should be, a computer teacher can seek out one classroom teacher who seems open to new ideas. Even if the teacher won't accompany students to the lab, if the computer teacher can get help in planning the technology lesson, the end product will at least parallel the learning that takes place in the classroom. Posting student projects in visible places sometimes energizes other teachers to request help in planning integrated lessons.

One computer teacher was successful when she asked the most collaborative teacher to attend for only the first ten minutes of lab so that the teacher could hear the expectations for students on the unit and could support it. This hooked that teacher so that she now attends the beginning of lab almost every week.

Over time, technology teachers should aim to help teachers begin to use technology in their classrooms. Giving teachers resources such as interactive Web sites or simple project ideas to support curricular content areas can spur some teachers to use technology on their own within the classroom.

Success breeds interest and more success. Often when one class has a particularly good experience, other teachers will ask to do similar projects. Even if they don't, what one class has done successfully can always be adapted for other classes at that grade level. Building a repertoire of successful projects enables a computer teacher to suggest ideas when teachers decide to try integrated lessons in their classrooms.

Creating a notebook of student samples can also provide an impetus for teachers. By looking through the notebook, a teacher will learn what skills the students have and will get ideas for ways to incorporate technology into the classroom. Additionally, principals and parents can leaf through the notebooks to learn how students are using technology.

The eventual goal for technology teachers is to hand off the responsibility for technology to classroom teachers so that the use of technology tools to support learning becomes the natural way of doing things, rather than an add-on.

The Classroom Teacher's Role in the Change Process

Teachers bear the primary responsibility for student use of technology. This may intimidate some teachers who either feel inadequate in their skills or uncertain of how to use technology as a tool to support learning. In fact, teachers often look for software titles to use in the classroom because students can work independently without knowing any technical skills.

As tempting as it is to use specialty software packages with students, no generic software package can possibly meet all students' needs appropriately. Software packages require teachers to adjust their instruction to the software's format rather than supporting the teachers' instructional methods. Instead of adjusting to someone else's style, teachers should consider how students can use technology to demonstrate what they have learned. Can students write reports? Create slide shows? Draw non-linguistic representations of concepts? Develop multimedia programs? Vary the final products so that students build skills in many applications. In late elementary, teachers may even offer choices for the final products so that students have even more buy-in to the content.

I don't mean to disparage all software and Web sites. In fact, sometimes an interactive Web site can reinforce a key idea of a unit better than a project will, and a software package will mesh perfectly with a skill being taught. However, some teachers place students on software with little connection to classroom instruction. That's a hard position to support because it devalues the use of technology from an instructional support to a babysitting tool.

Teachers unaccustomed to integrating technology with content knowledge might first choose a way for students to demonstrate what they've learned. Perhaps students can write stories that incorporate facts or letters from a character's viewpoint. Perhaps the unit lends itself to visual representation: pictures that illustrate poems, vocabulary words, or research projects. Slide shows to accompany oral presentations can meet multiple standards.

When the final product has been decided, the teacher estimates how long the project will take, including any research or instruction. After adding a couple of days to allow for interruptions, the teacher plans backward from the end date. The technology teacher can be helpful in estimating how long a project will take and can ensure that the students have the requisite skills to be successful.

Doing a project solo, especially as a first experience, requires great fortitude, Rather than bearing the pressure alone, a teacher can enlist help from a teaching partner, the technology teacher, parents, or even student peer coaches. The synergy of several minds will not only help teachers avoid pitfalls but will also improve the final product.

Finally, classroom teachers don't need to know all the skills for a project. Technology projects encourage students to practice problem solving. Students will figure out how to get around the barriers if the teacher can live with the discomfort of not having an immediate answer.

Technology integration supports differentiation among students. High-ability students often can produce more detailed or complex end products while struggling students may submit simplified products.

The classroom teacher is the *key* to successful integration. With support from an administrator and, if available, a technology teacher, classroom teachers can use technology tools to reinforce, extend, and assess students' understanding of curricular content. When technology is seamlessly integrated with classroom content instruction, students not only are more engaged in learning, but they also become better thinkers, planners, problem solvers, and citizens. Isn't that what teachers desire for all students?

<table>
<caption>Grade 1 Map
Trimester 1</caption>
<tr><th></th><th>8/18–8/20</th><th>8/23–8/27</th><th>8/30–9/3</th><th>9.6–9/10</th><th>9/13–9/17</th><th>9/20–9/24</th><th>9/27–10/1</th><th>10/4–10/8</th><th>10/11–10/15</th><th>10/18–10/22</th><th>10/25–10/29</th><th>11/1–11/5</th><th>11/8–11/12</th></tr>
<tr><td>Reading</td><td colspan="3">Assessments</td><td colspan="10">Mini-Lessons; Shared Reading; Guided Reading; Whole Group/Small Group Instruction; Read Alouds</td></tr>
<tr><td>Writing</td><td>Writing Sample</td><td colspan="4">Introduction to Writing</td><td colspan="8">Complete Sentences; Journals; Step Up to Writing</td></tr>
<tr><td>Math</td><td colspan="6">Chapter One</td><td colspan="5">Chapter Two</td><td colspan="2">Chapter Three</td></tr>
<tr><td>Social Studies</td><td colspan="3">My School</td><td colspan="4">Sportsmanship; Playground Safety</td><td colspan="4">Fire Safety</td><td colspan="2">Maps/Globes</td></tr>
<tr><td>Science</td><td></td><td colspan="2">Fall</td><td colspan="5">Insects</td><td colspan="5">Spiders; Pumpkins</td></tr>
<tr><td>Tech</td><td></td><td></td><td colspan="2">Insect Web sites: Digital Dragonflies</td><td colspan="2">Insect labeled pictures; Riddles</td><td colspan="2">Making number chart</td><td>Starfall reading Web site</td><td colspan="2">Spider squares; Splat squares; Counting by 2s and 5s</td><td colspan="2">Virtual Math Manipulatives</td></tr>
</table>

Chapter 3

Curricular Planning

TECHNOLOGY SHOULD NOT BE A SEPARATE CURRICULUM because it must support the core content areas. Yet teachers consistently ask, "What skills should I teach and when?"

I don't know the answer for anyone else's students. Technology skills should be taught when the learner has a reason to use them. Practicing skills for authentic purposes makes them meaningful and memorable.

In my district, teachers can take computer classes monthly. Some teachers have taken the same word processing class three and four times—and they are no better at word processing than when they began. Was the instruction poor? No, but the skills were not tied to specific needs, so the teachers had no reason to practice them. Large group instruction of skills that people will not use immediately has little staying power.

On the other hand, a colleague who wanted to track students' test results felt powerful when she learned how to make a table. For the next few days, she not only set up several tables for herself, but taught two other staff members how to create tables. She is now an expert on making tables!

The same is true for students. They need a reason to practice the skills they are being taught. Kindergarteners learn about Edit...Undo because they cry if they can't fix their mistakes. First graders learn to copy and paste because they have projects that require them to use those skills. Fourth and fifth graders learn about headers and footers because they create multi-page documents.

Not all students learn the same skills at the same time. Since a teacher's assessment of her own students' needs drives instruction, some projects are confined to only one class at a grade level. For instance, a second-grade teacher introduced desktop publishing as part of a unit on conventions in non-fiction. Her teammates had neither the need nor desire to use technology in that way. Does it matter that 25% of the second graders practiced desktop publishing and their classmates didn't? No. When the students are in fourth grade, all of them will have desktop publishing opportunities. Those with experience will become peer coaches for the inexperienced.

One Collaborative Model

In the mid-90s, the Library Power grants sponsored by the DeWitt Wallace Foundation encouraged a collaborative model in schools. Schools with grant funding received more than a hundred hours of staff development on how to integrate library research into classroom instruction. Using a form provided through the training, teachers and library media specialists planned research units that supported science and social studies curricula. During these units, the classroom teachers and librarian co-taught the skills and worked collaboratively to help students develop final products. In their evaluations after the units finished, the collaborators decided whether the unit should be repeated in successive years.

At Lenski, the collaborative model expanded over time to include the technology team. The library media specialist acted as a liaison at first to coordinate how technology would be included, but the partnership gradually became a triad of the

FIGURE 3.1 Collaborative planning drives instruction at Lenski. In this picture, the principal, library media specialist, and technology team are reviewing curriculum maps with grade-level teachers.

classroom teacher, library media specialist, and technology teacher. Depending on the timing of lab schedules, library availability, and classroom instruction, anyone on the team could introduce a unit. Students used technology to supplement research, take notes, and create final products.

Successful integration of technology with research units led to additional collaborations between the classroom teachers and technology team. While rarely formalized on planning sheets, the lessons follow the library integration model. Classroom teachers and technology teachers talk about curricular targets and students' needs and then create a plan for addressing the needs through an interactive program, a technology-based project, or another form of technology. As grade levels build a base of technology lessons, the planning takes less time. Almost ten years later, the collaborative model looks seamless to visitors.

In a school with little experience in collaboration, teachers would benefit from using planning forms. The collaborative planning form (See figure 3.2) could be used initially as a guideline. The advantage of a planning form is that it delineates who takes responsibility for each activity of the unit.

Collaborative Unit Planning Sheet

Teacher(s): Collaborative Partner(s):

Curricular Area(s): Content Target(s):

Standards Addressed:

Final Product:

Necessary Skills (Content, Technology, Information Literacy):

Timeline:

Date: Person Responsible: Activity:

Collaborative Unit Evaluation

Successes:

Suggested changes:

(Attach worksheets, rubrics, and sample finished projects.)

FIGURE 3.2 **COLLABORATIVE PLANNING AND EVALUATION SHEET**. During planning for a unit of shared responsibility, the classroom teacher, librarian, and technology teacher can identify the standards (state, information literacy, and NET•S) being addressed, the primary responsibilities of each team member, and the timeline of events. When the unit ends, the team can use the reverse side to capture any ideas for improvement. Keeping the completed planning sheets in a notebook in a central location speeds up planning in future years.

Tools for Collaborative Planning

The planning sheet is only one of several tools used for collaborative units. At the start of the school year, each grade-level team completes a yearlong curriculum map, which roughly outlines when they plan to teach curricular units in each content area. The original is a spreadsheet that is updated annually to reflect the new calendar. All support teachers receive copies of the maps to use in planning differentiated or supplemental lessons. In the first years of curriculum planning, the form addressed only the core content areas, but over time, the form has evolved to include planning for technology as well. While the map doesn't include all technology that will be used, it does outline the major projects that grade-level teachers know they want to include for the year.

Grade 1 Map
Trimester 1

	8/18–8/20	8/23–8/27	8/30–9/3	9.6–9/10	9/13–9/17	9/20–9/24	9/27–10/1	10/4–10/8	10/11–10/15	10/18–10/22	10/25–10/29	11/1–11/5	11/8–11/12
Reading	Assessments			Mini-Lessons; Shared Reading; Guided Reading; Whole Group/Small Group Instruction; Read Alouds									
Writing	Writing Sample	Introduction to Writing				Complete Sentences; Journals; Step Up to Writing							
Math	Chapter One						Chapter Two					Chapter Three	
Social Studies	My School			Sportsmanship; Playground Safety				Fire Safety				Maps/Globes	
Science		Fall		Insects					Spiders; Pumpkins				
Tech			Insect Web sites: Digital Dragonflies		Insect labeled pictures; Riddles		Making number chart		Starfall reading Web site	Spider squares; Splat squares; Counting by 2s and 5s		Virtual Math Manipulatives	

FIGURE 3.3 CURRICULUM PLANNING MAP. This page from a first-grade curriculum map shows the major units of study and the anticipated schedule for technology projects. Note that while the technology entries typically are general and subject to change, in October, each teacher designated a different specific activity for her class. Prior to getting LCD projectors, teachers used the lab to familiarize primary students with Web sites and software used as activity centers in the classroom, but now teachers can introduce those activities in the classroom, so more lab time is spent doing projects where having multiple adult helpers makes the work easier.

Additionally, all support teachers have copies of the district curricular targets for each grade level. These targets are based on the state standards. When the third grade begins a unit on the solar system, for instance, support teachers look at the targets to see the depth of understanding a typical student should reach. Technology projects, as well as special education and/or gifted-talented lessons, can be differentiated for struggling and advanced students based on the typical students' target.

	Grade 1 Targets
Language Arts	
Reading	Use terms related to print (period, exclamation point, question mark)
	Recognize terms related to book structure (cover, title, author, illustrator, title page, dedication)
	Recognize and apply structural analysis for single and plural words
	Recognize/Retell story elements (beginning, middle, end; characters, setting, plot, problems, resolution
	Recall important details of a story, sequence events, summarize
	Use illustrations to interpret text, review the material
	Draw conclusions and make inferences about characters or events
	Experience literature through read alouds, sharing reading, guided reading, independent reading
Writing	Use appropriate handwriting skills
	Write with practical/technical intent, including thank-you letters
	Write with expository intent, including written responses and reports
	Write with expressive/creative intent, including simple stories and poems
	Develop an awareness of spelling through print
	Use approximate spelling, including beginning, middle, and ending sounds
	Spell the first 35 core words correctly within own writing
	Proofread by searching for correct spelling of core words in charts, word finders, labels, books

FIGURE 3.4 DISTRICT GRADE-LEVEL TARGETS. With a spreadsheet of grade-level targets to consult, classroom teachers and support teachers know what specific skills related to a curricular unit to target for mastery. At the intermediate grades, where students are tested by the state in some core content areas, the state's assessment frameworks provide guidance about instructional targets as well.

At the end of the year, the technology teacher completes a similar curriculum map that outlines the technology program as it unfolded the previous year for each class at each grade level. During the next year's grade-level planning cycle, the year's overview helps the teachers remember the projects and lessons their classes did. Teachers can see which curricular areas need more emphasis, which lessons met curricular targets, and which lessons need to be tweaked or scrapped.

Grade 1 Tech Map
Trimester 3

	2/21–2/25	2/28–3/4	3/7–3/11	3/14–3/18	3/21–3/25	4/4–4/8	4/11–4/15	4/18–4/22	4/25–4/29	5/2–5/6
Reading			Starfall Plays –ME, C, MI	Starfall–MI						
Writing			Picture for Story Prompt –ME	Picture for Story Prompt –ME	Facts about Reptiles–MI	Write about Reptiles–C			Mother's Day Portrait–MI	Mother's Day Card and Picture –C, ME, MI
Math	Coin Critters–ME Comparing Numbers–C	Splat Squares–ME			Kids Tables and Time (Subtraction) –C	Coin Critters (Quarters) –ME	Fact Families (Paint)–C	Fact Families (Paint)–C	NLVM (Geoboards) –ME	NLVM (Geoboards) –MI
Social Studies	George Washington –ME, MI									
Science	Zoobooks–V	Food Riddles –C, ME Zoobook web site–V	Write Food Riddles –C, MI Food Riddles –V	Croc Photos –C, V Reptile Word Search–MI	Reptile Word Search –ME, MI Picture of Reptile–ME	Draw Reptile –C. MI Reptile Word Search–V	Paint Water Cycle –ME, MI Crocodile Word Search –V			

C=Cole, V=Vyhnalek, ME=Metherd, MI-Miller

FIGURE 3.5 TECHNOLOGY CURRICULUM REPORT. This tech map shows a sample of the technology lessons worked on in the computer lab over the past year. Lessons are placed according to the content areas they supported. Note the variety of each week's lessons. During summer curriculum planning, teachers refer to this map to evaluate what they need to change. In this Trimester 3 page, for instance, teachers may consider whether they need to increase the technology support for social studies content.

The technology team also uses this tool to create a vision for the following year. Are there essential skills that should be added? Were any lessons too ambitious for the developmental skills of a grade level?

The final tool in this chapter, a scope and sequence chart, is included reluctantly. This chart seems to answer the question of what to teach and when. However, because we believe that students should learn skills on an as-needed basis, we do not use this chart for planning. After completing the end-of-the-year technology map that lists the year's computer lab lessons, we revise the scope and sequence chart. The chart then reflects the skills students learned in the previous year.

The chart serves as a *review* of the past year, *not a guideline* for the future. When a teacher wants to know whether her new class has practiced a particular computer skill, the scope and sequence chart provides an answer. Note that this chart is not specific for individual teachers. If more than 50% of the students at the grade level have been taught a skill, the scope and sequence chart reflects it. If fewer than 50% have experience with a skill, then the chart does not include it for that grade level. Because students are shuffled for class placement each year and we receive new students with little technology background, having 50% of students experienced in a skill provides sufficient peer coaches for using the skills in a project.

The scope and sequence chart is based on ISTE's National Educational Technology Standards for students (NETS•S), but it is a year's review, not a prescriptive plan. Still, Trecie and I do pay attention to at least meeting the standards annually, so that Lenski students develop technology proficiency over time. Throughout the year, we keep mental tabs on the skills introduced at each grade level. When a teacher gets 'stuck' on only one form of technology, such as word processing, for all projects, we gently advocate a different type of experience in the next unit. Each grade level should expose students to new skills and new technologies, so that students build competencies with various applications.

TABLE 3.1 **LENSKI SCOPE AND SEQUENCE CHART.** This chart represents the previous year's coverage of skills with students.

I=Introduction D=Developing M=Mastery						
Standard 1: Students will demonstrate a sound understanding of the nature and operation of technology systems and are proficient in the use of technology.	**K**	**1**	**2**	**3**	**4**	**5**
Identify parts of the computer	I	D	M	M	M	M
Use CDs properly	I	D	M	M	M	M
Use computer terms: menu, icon, scroll bar, cursor, etc.	I	D	M	M	M	M
Turn on/off a computer properly	I	D	M	M	M	M
Log in with user name and password		I	D	M	M	M

	K	1	2	3	4	5
Use mouse skills (single-, double-right/left clicks)	I	D	M	M	M	M
Launch/close applications on hard drive and CDs	I	M	M	M	M	M
Save/retrieve work from desktop files	I	M				
Save/retrieve work on a network			I	D	M	M
Save/retrieve work with flash drive and/or CD burner					I	D
Use Internet bookmarks, navigate a site	I	D	M	M	M	M
Locate/use basic keyboard keys, such as enter, space bar, shift, arrows, backspace, etc.	I	D	M	M	M	M
Keyboarding: correct side of keyboard, home row		I	D	M	M	M
Keyboarding: correct fingering, posture, touch typing			I	D	D	D
Handle a wireless laptop appropriately			I	D	M	M
Troubleshoot wireless connectivity issues				I	D	D
Standard 2: Students will understand ethical, cultural, and societal issues related to technology. They will practice responsible use of technology systems, information, and software. They will develop positive attitudes toward technology uses that support lifelong learning, collaboration, personal pursuits, and productivity.	K	1	2	3	4	5
Describe uses of technology in society			I	D	D	D
Demonstrate proper usage of equipment (computers and peripherals)	I	D	M	M	M	M
Understand/adhere to copyright laws				I	D	D
Understand/adhere to hardware and software licensing agreements					I	D
Understand/adhere to district and school procedures	I	D	M	M	M	M
Work cooperatively and collaboratively with others when using technology	I	D	M	M	M	M
Practice safe searching and communications techniques				I	D	D

Standard 3: Students will use technology tools to enhance learning, increase productivity, and promote creativity. They will use productivity tools to collaborate in constructing technology-enhanced models, prepare publications, and produce other creative works.	K	1	2	3	4	5
Word-processing skills:						
Enter/delete text	I	D	M	M	M	M
Select text/format with font options		I	D	M	M	M
Edit alignment/justification, line spacing, and margins				I	D	M
Cut/copy/paste within or between documents		I	D	M	M	M
Undo/redo	I	D	M	M	M	M
Use spell check			I	D	M	M
Import/manipulate graphics (clip art, drawings, digital camera images, saved images)			I	M	M	M
Use Word Art and add page borders			I	M	M	M
Use Save As		I	D	D	M	M
Find/replace			I	D	M	M
Insert, position, remove tabs						I
Use the thesaurus and definitions				I	D	M
Use text boxes with format options			I	D	M	M
Add headers and footers			I	D	M	M
Print (select printer, set number of copies)		I	D	M	M	M
Use printing options (two-sided printing, color choices)					I	D
Graphics:						
Access/use drawing program (tools, text)	I	D	M	M	M	M
Manipulate a graphic		I	D	M	M	M
Use the scanner and digital camera			I	D	D	M
Search for, locate, download, and save non-copyrighted images from the Internet			I	D	D	M
Insert graphics into other applications		I	M	M	M	M

Standard 4: Students use telecommunications to collaborate, publish, and interact with peers, experts, and other audiences. Students use a variety of media and formats to communicate information and ideas effectively to multiple audiences.	K	1	2	3	4	5
E-mail:						
Retrieve/send an e-mail message					I	D
Reply to/forward/delete an e-mail					I	D
Add to an address book					I	D
Copy/paste word processing to/from an e-mail message					I	D
Multimedia presentations:						
Start/open a presentation			I	D	M	M
Format a master slide				I	D	M
Add text and graphics to slides			I	M	M	M
Add transitions to slides					D	M
Add sound effects and/or video/music					I	D
Use various View options (show, slide sorter, etc.)			I	D	M	M
Insert a hyperlink in a slide						D
Communicate through a series of slides			I	D	D	D
Desktop publications:						
Create a brochure, newsletter, book, or flyer		I	D	D	M	M
Add graphics and text		D	M	M	M	M
Apply design principles to layout and font					D	M
Blogs, discussion boards, collaborative document sites:						
Post appropriate materials to a Web-based collaborative site					I	D
Respond appropriately to the postings of others					I	D

Standard 5: Students use technology to locate, evaluate, and collect information from a variety of sources. Students use technology tools to process data and report results. Students evaluate and select new information resources and technological innovations based on the appropriateness for specific tasks.	K	1	2	3	4	5
Gather reference material from an online database			I	D	M	M
Identify key words, names, and phrases for a search		I	D	M	M	M
Access a Web site by typing a URL				D	M	M
Search using a Web browser			I	D	M	M
Evaluate search results from a search engine				I	D	D
Use a Web browser toolbar	D	M	M	M	M	M
Capture information from an online source and transfer text to a word processor					I	D
Capture and save graphics				I	D	M
Use proper citation methods for sources and pictures			I	D	D	D
Upload and download files and programs, as appropriate					I	D

Standard 6: Students use technology resources for solving problems and making informed decisions. Students employ technology in the development of strategies for solving problems in the real world.	K	1	2	3	4	5
Recognize the elements of a spreadsheet			I	D	M	M
Enter text and numbers, move among cells			I	D	M	M
Format a cell or block of cells						I
Insert data in a data table	I	D	M	M	M	M
Create a data table			I	D	D	M
Create an appropriate graph from a data table	I	D	M	M	M	M
Format graph (background, font, text color, etc.)			I	D	M	M
Add header/footer			I	I	D	D
Interpret spreadsheet results			I	D	D	D
Copy/paste a graph into other applications			I	D	D	D
Create a chronological timeline				I	D	D

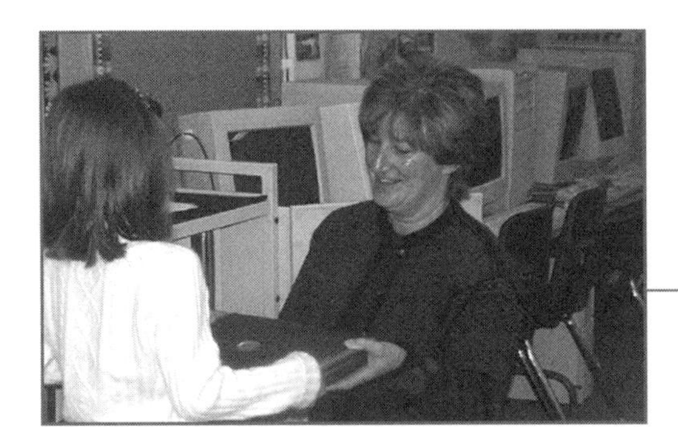

Chapter 4

Acquiring Technology on a Limited Budget

COORDINATING TECHNOLOGY USE WITHIN A SCHOOL OR SCHOOL DISTRICT requires two vastly different sets of skills: *instructional* and *technical*. Few people will have both kinds of skills, and managing either the instructional or technical aspects of a technology program poses significant challenges.

The *instructional* responsibility refers to how students and teachers use technology to support, reinforce, and assess students' learning. Most of this book addresses instructional technology skills at the elementary school level. It represents a paradigm shift because it proposes that schools move away from treating technology as an add-on toward integrating technology seamlessly into instruction. This chapter addresses the technical challenges of making the shift.

The *technical* side encompasses acquiring and maintaining equipment, managing networks, and providing tools for administrative efficiency such as accounting and student information systems. For schools to change the way they use technology, students and administrators need adequate access to computers and other tools. Providing such access has been an on-going struggle for most districts and schools.

Schools that have strong district support on the equipment side of technology can skip this chapter. However, for schools lacking adequate equipment and the technical skills to build less expensive environments, this chapter will provide models in use by schools around the world.

Information Technology Services (ITS) professionals in education typically recommend that districts and schools follow a business-style purchase/lease plan that replaces 25–35% of computers annually as a regular budget line. With such a plan, school districts can ensure that the computers are under warranty (removing the need for district-level maintenance) and are continually upgraded.

This philosophy makes sense. ITS departments in districts and schools generally are stretched thin to manage the infrastructure, administrative needs for data management, and school needs. Acquiring new computers under warranty essentially outsources maintenance, and regular replacement keeps school equipment up-to-date. When districts can adhere to this model, they free schools to focus on instructional uses of technology.

However, lack of consistent funding has reduced the number of districts that can adhere to a regular replacement schedule. In my district, because of the lack of funding, only a few teacher/administrator computers are being replaced annually. At Lenski, with 70 staff members, the district has provided fewer than 30 teacher/administrator computers and no student computers in six years. That places the burden for acquiring equipment on schools.

Many schools face this dilemma, particularly in states in the bottom quarter of per pupil spending and in small or rural districts. In these schools, students may use nine- to ten-year-old computers with no prospect of replacement in the near future. While to wealthier districts, the equipment seems hopelessly outdated, teachers who have no other options learn to make the best of what they have.

The inability to manage a replacement plan means that schools often lack adequate equipment to provide rich technology experiences for students. No wonder teachers resist changing the ways they use technology!

Creative thinking can overcome these obstacles. This chapter will outline three models for providing sufficient computer access to students with minimal financial outlay. These models are currently being successfully implemented at schools.

Refurbished Computers

Instead of buying or leasing new computers under warranty and trying to replace them regularly, a school or district could contract with a refurbishing company to lease or buy used computers with warranties. These computers typically come from

RESOURCES

PCs for Schools

Computers for Schools (www.pcsforschools.org), the first Microsoft Authorized Refurbisher, takes donations from businesses and refurbishes them for schools and other non-profits. Their customers pay about one-third the cost of a new computer, just enough to cover the refurbishing costs, and get a three-year warranty at no extra cost. Computers for Schools (CFS) has offices in Chicago and Philadelphia, but works with schools across the nation. According to Willie Cade, president and CEO of CFS, the failure rate of refurbished computers is less than nine percent, which is much lower than the failure rate of new computers.

FIGURE 4.1 In September 2005, the School District of Philadelphia awarded a contract to CFS to provide 3,000 refurbished computers with three-year warranties over three years.

large corporations who use them for two to three years and then sell them to a refurbisher. The refurbishing company replaces unreliable parts, cleans the machines, and reformats the hard drives.

A refurbisher can generally sell a large number of identical computers that look like new and carry three- or four-year warranties for 40% less than new computers. The warranties cover most maintenance issues, so a school or district still does not need a large technical support staff, yet students and administrators have access to computers with sufficient power to run most current applications. The reduced prices help schools and districts stretch their dollars farther.

The greatest disadvantage to this model is that it still requires a significant outlay of cash. Additionally, high school students and staff may need more power than older computers offer. At the elementary school, much student work doesn't require lightning speed or large amounts of memory, so this model will work.

This model is the easiest of the three to implement because it is so similar to the popular business model that many schools and districts have tried to follow.

The Thin Client Model

The K–12 Linux Terminal Server Project (K12LTSP) and Skolelinux are computer hardware and support models being deployed around the world because both are so cost-effective. Thin client models can be implemented with older computers and a fast server. All software is provided free of charge by the open source community, and the software includes all the components needed for a school. Schools do not have to pay any licensing fees and often can use older machines no longer usable as Windows machines.

The Rocky Mountain School of Expeditionary Learning (RMSEL), a magnet school that serves six school districts in the Denver metro area, uses K12LTSP to run two servers donated by IBM and about 100 student computers. The student machines are "thin clients," or shells, with processors, memory, and network cards but no hard drives. While it appears to students as though they are working on the computers in front of them, these workstations are actually continually accessing programs running on the server. The number of client computers served by one server depends on the processing speed and memory cache of the server.

To set up a thin client design, a school would need one or more fast computers with large hard drives to act as servers. In 2006, these servers would probably cost about $2000 each. One server can generally handle about 100 terminals simultaneously, although the transfer speed slows as the server reaches maximum capacity. The workstations (terminals) can be any computers with Pentium I processors or better. Pentium processors were introduced in 1993, so a school could use very old machines.

The software for either K12LTSP (www.k12ltsp.org) or Skolelinux (www.skolelinux.org/portal/) can be downloaded from Web sites or ordered on CDs. The software includes all the applications for server management and student use.

While the following is not an exhaustive list, it demonstrates the versatility of tools included in the software package: Nautilus or Konqueror for file management; Mozilla, Opera, or Lynx for Web browsing; KMail or Ximian Evolution for e-mail; and OpenOffice or K Office for productivity software. Additionally, the open source community has created free educational software such as Tux Type and Tux Math. A typical ITS staff member can easily load the software and configure the network, especially since the users' groups maintain active discussion areas on the Web site.

The thin client model has many advantages for the technical support staff:

1. Most maintenance is done at the server, not at individual computers. Because the workstations are thin clients, or shells, maintenance generally consists of replacing a monitor or keyboard. However, the server is a true computer with heavy demands on its components, so a component may fail.
2. Upgrades are loaded only on the server(s). Because the computers depend on the server(s) for all software, once the server is upgraded, the entire system is working from that upgrade.
3. Linux is extremely hardy. Schools and businesses have been known to go longer than a year without rebooting their servers. Other operating systems need to be rebooted weekly and sometimes daily, or they bog down.
4. Linux is far less susceptible to viruses than other operating systems. Because the operating system is built with security as a primary consideration, protection is built-in, not an additional licensed software service.
5. All of the software is free. Open-source software is free, so a school can load the thin client protocol at no cost—no licensing fees, no additional security services, no contracts with vendors unless they choose to pay a vendor for support services.

Additionally, software such as Open Office can read and write files to be used in other proprietary software such as Microsoft Office. Students can work on projects at home even if the home computer has other software.

An IT director would need to weigh the disadvantages as well:

1. If the server crashes, no one can do any work until the server is repaired. Since every workstation depends on the server, nothing can be done without access to the server. A back-up server would mitigate this problem.
2. Specialty software already owned by a school may not run on the server. Many specialty software packages were built to work with Windows and Macintosh operating systems, not Linux. The server may need to run an open-source software package that can mimic the Windows environment.
3. An overloaded network will run slowly. While the software can handle many clients, the network and server have limits on what they will run efficiently. A lab of 35 thin clients will run smoothly; 150 thin clients will require more than one server.
4. The servers cost money. While the expense for servers is minimal compared to buying student workstations, it is not negligible. Rarely will someone donate a computer sufficiently new, fast, and powerful enough to run a thin client network. However, schools do not need to buy overpriced servers either. Good computers will work as servers.

The Lenski Model

At Lenski Elementary, we experimented with the K12LTSP model, but because of district guidelines concerning the use of Windows, it didn't make sense for us to adopt it. Instead, we initiated a program of refurbishing donated computers, recruiting volunteer technical support, and creating software tools that would make management of the network easier for administrators who were not technically adept.

First, we solicited donations of outdated computers from local businesses through a letter sent to mid-sized companies. We offered to take any computer equipment that was still usable but no longer useful to them. Companies responded quickly; donating to us saved them the recycling fees, and qualified as a donation to a non-profit.

When it became clear that we could not process the donations quickly enough, my husband and I launched Teen Tech, a volunteer program for high school teens and community members. We invited students from the local high schools to volunteer 3.5 hours one night a week to refurbish computers and learn technical skills. The high schools supported this opportunity by offering independent study credit for the students, provided we documented their volunteer hours.

We then spread the word about the program to computer hobbyists in the community. The adults who responded typically were professionals in computer science fields who had an interest in open-source software, such as Linux. They were attracted by our desire to incorporate open-source software as much as possible.

Because of district guidelines, all computers in the schools run the Windows operating system and Microsoft Office software suite. However, we opted to use Linux on all servers and to incorporate open-source software such as Tux Paint and Tux Type. We also found a variety of free educational programs for PCs.

At first the high school students spent most of their time refurbishing donated computers, but they were so efficient that, within four months, we had filled the classrooms and labs with as many computers as the staff could handle. Still, the students kept building usable computers. We built a second computer lab in our school and provided a lab of thin clients to the Rocky Mountain School of Expeditionary Learning. Eventually, we found other schools eager to have refurbished computers.

The number of donations surprised us. In six years, we have sent solicitation letters twice. Otherwise, word of mouth has kept donations coming, and we have been able to refresh all the original donated computers at least once. In five years, we estimate that we have refurbished more than 500 computers!

In 2006, the donations began to include Pentium IV laptops as well as desktops and LCD monitors. This has allowed us to replace bulky desktop computers in classrooms with smaller laptops, even though their waning battery life requires the laptops to be plugged in all the time.

Passing Along Opportunity

The first family to receive a free computer through Team Tech showed up on a snowy winter evening. Mom and Dad, tentative smiles fixed on their faces, entered the library hesitantly with the teacher who had urged them to take advantage of the offer for their children's sake. Fifth-grader Pedro and his younger sister bounced ahead of their parents, barely able to restrain from running. Neither said much while the teacher introduced everyone, but their impatience showed in their jitteriness and the frequent glances they cast at the computer set up on a library table. One volunteer fluent in Spanish stepped forward to invite the family to the computer. Pedro slid into the seat and started pushing buttons.

"Slow down, Pedro," the teacher said, "until you know what they want you to do."

In no time, Pedro had discovered the free games included in the distribution, along with Open Office, which his teacher assured him could be used to finish schoolwork. While he and his sister explored the desktop and applications, the volunteer answered the parents' questions. Eventually, Pedro shut the computer down so that he and his parents could practice attaching the cords to set up the computer at home. The cords had been color-coded to simplify the process, but the family practiced several times so that they wouldn't have trouble once they reached home.

The family also practiced turning on and shutting down the computer. The parents watched Pedro, but neither tried to handle the mouse or experiment with the computer. They were clearly inexperienced with computers and worried about looking incompetent. After less than an hour, the family was ready to depart with the computer.

The volunteers ask about Pedro regularly, and his teacher says he and his sister talk about how much they use the computer at home.

Since that first family, Team Tech has refurbished computers for numerous families from Pedro's school and from Lenski and neighboring schools. So far, in only one case has a parent sat down to use the computer in our presence; yet, we've heard that soon after the computers are set up in their homes, parents ask their children how to use the programs and games. Most of these families do not have land phone lines, so Internet use is not possible, but becoming familiar with basic computer applications prepares them for future opportunities in their jobs.

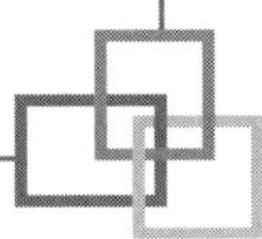

Additionally, the cadre of volunteers has written software tools for administrative tasks such as turning the Internet on and off, clearing the printer queue, and generating student accounts and passwords. Volunteers also troubleshoot technical problems, make and run Ethernet cables, and upgrade software.

Because donations continue to come in more frequently than Lenski can deploy them, the volunteer program, now called Team Tech, is refurbishing donated computers for needy families. The computers run open-source software, which is often unfamiliar to families, so the volunteers also teach the families how to set up and run their computers.

Lenski's model is not right for everyone. It requires flexibility, time, and many willing volunteers. The person in charge of the donations program needs to acquire the donations, recruit volunteers, and supervise the work. The donations come in irregularly, so some weeks will be hectic and some fairly quiet. In many schools, the district ITS department may be uncomfortable about who will manage the new equipment, so the person in charge may need to assure in writing that ITS will not be required to service donated computers. However, managed correctly, such a program can provide your school or district with as many computers as your students can use.

Consider the following advantages of this model:

1. Schools develop partnerships with businesses, which often prefer donating excess equipment to schools rather than paying a company to recycle them.
2. Schools can acquire newer and reasonably fast computers that cost only the sweat equity to pick up the computers from the donor and refurbish the donations for the school.
3. Schools can choose whether to use the operating system originally loaded on the computers or an open-source operating system. This provides more flexibility in deciding how to configure computers for students.
4. When a server fails, the computers continue to work. While a server failure may make some services inaccessible, such as Internet or accessing server folders, students can still work on the computers.
5. Schools can increase their visibility in the community by providing volunteer opportunities to teens and community members. Computer hobbyists rarely volunteer in schools because they do not realize how valued their talents would be. Not one of the community volunteers in our program has a child in our school, or even in our district! We consider this a public relations opportunity to promote public education.
6. When the school's technology needs are met, a volunteer group can provide computers for the community's needy citizens.

A donations program has disadvantages as well:

1. Computers are not standardized. We take all brands, which means they come apart differently and require different drivers. This adds a layer of complexity to refurbishing and troubleshooting.
2. All upgrades have to be loaded on each computer separately. Upgrading software takes time that teachers often don't have. Fortunately, this is an appropriate task for the volunteer force and is even fun when five or six people work together.
3. Student workstations are more likely to fail because they are stand-alone computers. When a school has too few computers already, a failed hard drive can significantly disrupt a teacher's lesson plan, but with a donations program, schools can keep extras in reserve to replace a problem computer quickly.

4. This model requires lots of sweat equity and flexibility. Schools have an option of spending money or time. This model requires time and a ready supply of committed volunteers.

When schools face on-going budget shortfalls and have a vision for integrating technology, they need creative approaches to acquiring and maintaining computers. While these three models are not the only answers, they do work, as evidenced by the schools that use them successfully now. Over the past few years, open-source software has become more user-friendly, and as stewards of public monies, schools should at least explore whether an open-source solution would work for them.

Other Technology Equipment

Until recently, Lenski had received only desktop computers from corporations, but in the past year, businesses are donating laptops as well. Even if the donated laptops need to be plugged in constantly because their batteries will no longer hold a charge, they take less space and produce less heat in classrooms, a clear benefit.

Lenski has yet to acquire an interactive whiteboard or LCD projector from a company, but those products may enter the donation cycle soon, and the school is definitely interested. One parent has suggested that older handheld PCs may also become more widely available soon. Although Lenski does not currently use handhelds, some teachers have expressed interest in using them, so we wouldn't turn them down if they were offered.

Digital cameras are now so inexpensive that families will often donate their older models when they buy newer ones. Provided the cameras have USB download capability, these enhance the technology programs at schools. Putting digital cameras in the hands of students to record field trips and collaborative projects gives them practice with 21st-century tools. If a donated camera gets broken by accident, the loss is less traumatic than the loss of a camera purchased from the school's budget.

However, Lenski consistently declines printer donations. Many businesses and families have older printers for disposal or donation. In our experience, these rarely work well enough to warrant accepting them. Additionally, schools need high-volume printers to handle the load. A company's high-volume printer has generally reached the end of its useful life, and families don't purchase high-volume printers. In my first year at Lenski, troubleshooting printing problems took 75% of my time, so ever since then, I have firmly believed in buying good, networked, high-capacity printers and placing them strategically around the building.

Lenski also declines donated scanners. For some reason, our elementary students find scanners more difficult to learn than computers or digital cameras, so we chose to buy several identical, inexpensive scanners. Besides, finding the drivers for multiple brands of scanners challenges even a skilled technical crew.

RESOURCES

Free and Almost Free Software for Elementary Schools

Small educational programs can be found at little or no cost to schools. Freeware can be used as an activity center in the classroom as well as a supplemental activity in the lab. When students finish their work faster than their classmates, using educational freeware builds skills while it keeps students busy.

This list of freeware and budget software highlights only a few programs. Additional sidebars in later chapters cover application-specific software that schools can use. The following are some of my favorite sites for budget software that works well in schools:

Owl and Mouse Software (www.yourchildlearns.com/owlmouse.htm): For PCs only, this site has a variety of programs, including many programs for pre- and emergent readers. For intermediate to middle school students, the site offers map puzzles. When Lenski's fourth graders study the United States, they enjoy racing the clock to match capitals with states.

Sebran's ABC and Minisebran (www.wartoft.nu/software/sebran/): Released under the GNU license, the program is currently only available for PCs, but the programmer mentions on the site that she hopes someone will convert it to Macintosh and Linux formats. The program has letter recognition and sounds, counting and equations, and simple typing recognition. The graphics appeals to primary students.

2+2 Math for Kids (www.funnymathforkids.com/about_program.php?jzk=eng/): This freeware program focuses on math for primary students. Each section has several different activities that support classroom math instruction. Depending on the aptitude of students, some activities may be appropriate as high as third grade. From counting to division, this freeware program offers a number of math activities that make practicing math facts fun.

ReadPlease 2003 (www.readplease.com): ReadPlease 2003 is a free abridged version of ReadPlease Plus 2003. Both programs download, but during the installation process, installers can choose to install only the freeware version. This program for PCs reads text aloud, a function built into Macs. Students can copy and paste their own typed text or any text from a Web site into ReadPlease and hear it read aloud. Beginning in second grade at Lenski, students learn to use the program independently whenever they need to hear text in a document or Web page read aloud. This is a wonderful way to edit word-processed work and to make Web text written above a students' reading level more accessible. This site now offers voice downloads for several European languages as well.

Grey Olltwit's Software (www.greyolltwit.com): Grey Olltwit's software used to be free, but his site now requires a one-time membership fee. Memberships cost $19.95 in 2006, which seems reasonable for the 37 educational programs and numerous games available to members. Site licenses are slightly higher, but still less expensive than most software programs.

Ray's Educational Software (www.rayslearning.com/index.htm): Students at Lenski use the *Tables and Time* software regularly to practice counting and math fact skills. Users can set options such as how high the numbers should go, whether to use a timer, and whether to play against the computer or another student. Spelling games are also available with the option of adding personal spelling lists. A site license for one program cost $68.00 in 2006.

Schools that accept donated technology equipment need to set clear standards for what they will and will not accept. No school has room to be the dumping ground for obsolete equipment, and disposal of many technology tools costs the district. Clear guidelines and targeted requests for equipment will help a school meet the technology needs of students without turning the school into a junkyard.

Funding Through Other Sources

Not everything at Lenski has been donated. I pursued every grant I could find and several paid for technology equipment.

The largest grant, a three-year Technology Grant from Plan for Social Excellence (www.pfse.org), paid for staff development, particularly conferences, and for about 100 computers. The Curriculum Innovation Team (CIT), a committee of teachers responsible for making decisions about the grant money and next steps in technology for Lenski, spent the first year's money on laptops for teachers. Every licensed teacher and many teacher assistants received the laptops for year-round use. What a difference that made in their personal use of technology! Teachers taught one another skills, experimented with applications at home where family members could help, and used their laptops in staff development trainings.

In the second year, the CIT bought three wireless laptop carts, the first in the district. Each cart had 15 wireless laptops, which was enough for one person to push and, we learned, sufficient for most classrooms because not all students needed laptops at the same time. The third year of the Technology Grant provided funds for an additional laptop cart and staff development.

Other grants have paid for LCD projectors, document cameras, and digital cameras for every classroom, two additional wireless carts, and AlphaSmart word processors. Some grants have been district or state sponsored, but small grants from foundations have helped as well. Unfortunately, most of the foundation grants that Lenski won have changed their programs and are no longer available to schools. In fact, finding money for technology has grown increasingly difficult.

Schools with access to new equipment and strong support from district ITS departments probably don't need to pursue alternative programs for acquiring equipment. However, those who lack the resources to provide adequate access to technology for students might consider whether even a slight change to their current systems, such as adopting an open-source application for an application that currently carries an annual licensing fee, could allow the district to repurpose some funding already in the budget.

RESOURCES

Portable Word Processors

Portable word processors provide an inexpensive tool for students who simply need to type, although many word processors today also offer wireless connections to the Internet. Although prices for laptops are coming down, portable word processors still offer a good value for schools with limited funds. Students with fine motor skill problems can use portable word processors in place of pencils and paper. In some schools, students can also check out the word processors overnight either to catch up on work or as an incentive to write.

AlphaSmart (www.alphasmart.com): AlphaSmart offers two options for schools: the Neo, a $249 portable word processor; and the Dana, a $429 wireless device with Palm OS and many software applications.

FIGURE 4.2 AlphaSmart products are highly durable for student use. The Neo is a typical word processor, while the Dana is geared toward the low-end laptop or handheld markets.

The Writer Learning System (www.writerlearning.com): Priced between $179 and $210, depending on add-ons, the Writer is competitively priced for standard word processing. The Writer offers several options geared toward special education students, including word prediction and voice recognition software.

QuickPad (www.quickpad.com): Priced at $199, QuickPad comes with word prediction and keyboarding applications pre-installed.

FIGURE 4.3 QuickPad appears similar to both the Neo and Writer word processors. It can hold ten different student accounts and these can be password protected.

Chapter 5

Infrastructure, Organization, and Logistics

WITHOUT ORGANIZATION, THE ABUNDANCE OF EQUIPMENT AT LENSKI and the heavy teaching load could easily overwhelm a technology resource teacher. Everything needs to be well organized—the technology infrastructure, the arrangement of teaching and learning spaces, the pacing and flow of lessons, and the logistics of supplying the most appropriate equipment when and where it's needed. Technology is more than just computers; it's a host of related peripherals and equipment that often seems to proliferate overnight. We learned early on that sharing the responsibility for organizing and managing the technology equipment and learning spaces was the only efficient way to run a vibrant program like Lenski's.

Infrastructure

My decision to solicit donated computers, and my principal's support of the idea, put Lenski in a precarious position for a while. I had been unaware that the district ITS guidelines forbade putting non-standard computers (which, in our case, meant any not purchased new from Dell) on the network. Yet, without donated computers, Lenski could not provide adequate access to technology for students or teachers.

We worked out a compromise with the district ITS department. The guidelines were revised to allow donated computers on the network provided the ITS department was not asked to provide technical support for any donated equipment. This created an inequity of sorts; schools with the expertise to repair equipment began gathering it from outside groups. Those without the expertise had to find the funding to purchase or lease new computers. The Lenski Team Tech group sponsored several workshops on troubleshooting hardware problems, replacing failed parts such as CD and hard drives, and making cables. Embedded in every workshop was the caveat that computer coaches could work only on donated equipment and not on computers under warranty.

Servers for student and teacher accounts also required a compromise. Schools typically purchased new, expensive Windows servers every three years and paid license fees. Because schools often shared servers, the ITS department limited the sizes of student and teacher accounts and insisted that students and teachers regularly purge files. Schools complained that the limits on account sizes meant teachers and students were often running out of space and losing time while they debated over what files to purge.

The Lenski technology team proposed loading open-source software on older donated computers to build stable servers with no licensing fees. This would provide enough capacity on the servers to allow students and teachers unlimited file space. Routing as much traffic as possible within the building would also speed up response times. The district's networking expert said that Lenski's plan did not compromise district security and, in fact, kept a lot of traffic off the district's network.

Using some of the first donated computers, my husband and I designed a server environment for Lenski's internal network. For all servers and firewalls, we now use a Mandrake distribution of Linux software. In addition to the modified firewall, we set up servers for file storage, backing up files, managing printing, and caching Web pages.

To add a layer of security to the wireless carts funded through the Technology Grant from Plan for Social Excellence, we have created a second separate network and placed a second network card in the file server. This gives students access to their files and the printers from the wireless network but restricts wireless Internet access. Only Lenski-registered wireless computers have access to the Internet and their use is limited to school hours on school days. During holidays and outside of school hours, the Internet is not available wirelessly from Lenski.

While teacher computers use dynamic IP addresses, student computers have static addresses that contain the room number where they are located (i.e., 172.16.12.3, where 12 designates the room number and 3 means the third computer from the door). This enables us to use scripts, written by the tech volunteers, to turn Internet access on and off to student machines by room number. Teachers request Internet access according to their ability to supervise students' use of the Internet. If teachers are able to constantly supervise their students on computers, then their computers can be connected all the time. If teachers don't want the worry about students using the Web inappropriately, then they ask for Internet access only when they need it.

Creating a file server allows us to give each student and teacher a unique log-on. What lessons we have learned from that! The first year, we gave every student and teacher common user names: the initial letter of the first name combined with the entire last name. My daughter Jamie keyed in 600+ user names and ID numbers with higher than 99% accuracy (bless her!). As soon as students started using these log-ons, we realized the advantage gained by someone with a short last name such as Lee or Smith over the person with a long, hyphenated name such as Oblinger-Martinez. The knowledge came too late to be fixed for that year, but we began immediately to work on another scheme.

In Year 2, we extracted students' names, ID numbers, and classroom teachers from the student information system and, using a script developed by the volunteers, converted the data to user names with the same format (initial of first name combined with last name). This time, we truncated each name at 6 characters, but then too many students ended up with the same user names (Abbie Montagne, Andrew Montague, and Allen Montana were all amonta), so we had to add a number at the end (amonta1, amonta2, amonta3). When many students struggled to remember where to truncate their names, we realized that we needed to revise our plan again.

The current scheme works better, although it, too, has difficulties. We extract student information from the student information system and use the same script to generate the user names and passwords. Now the user name is the student's first name and a number. With a few exceptions, such as when students go by their middle names or a nickname, this system works. Almost all students know how to spell their first names and they gain proficiency over several years. The number behind the name, such as andrew8, remains the same throughout the six years of elementary school.

The district does not currently support student e-mail, and the online e-mail services we have used have not allowed us to choose our own user names and passwords, but we would advocate using the same protocol at the elementary level for e-mail as well.

Organizing the Lab and Classroom

Some schools have moved away from using computer labs in favor of placing computers in the classrooms. Schools seem to have mixed results with this choice. When teachers have access to a professional who can demonstrate integrated lessons and help teachers build their skills, then the programs are often successful. When classroom teachers feel overwhelmed by the responsibility and don't see good role models who can help them with ideas and management, then many teachers limit their integration to using the Internet for research.

Lenski chooses to maintain a lab for several reasons. First, we have sufficient computers for the classrooms, so we don't have to choose between placing computers in a lab or classrooms. With access to the lab, classroom computers, and more than 100 wireless laptops, teachers can use computers whenever and however they wish.

Second, we find that the youngest students gain skills faster when they all can try them at once. In a lab, we can demonstrate a drawing program and release all the students to practice the skills on a project simultaneously. Then when they return to their classrooms they can work as pairs or singly on classroom computers without the need for re-teaching the skills. Kindergarten and first-grade teachers are least likely to use the laptops. The time necessary for set-up, monitoring, troubleshooting, and cleaning up makes the use of laptops inefficient in those classrooms.

Third, the lab lowers class size temporarily. Intermediate-level teachers often use lab time for writing and other projects that require intensive adult support. With three or four adults in the room, students get much more attention, whether they are conducting research, working with text, or encountering technical problems.

Finally, using a lab encourages collaboration and accountability. Classroom teachers have instant partners for planning units and projects when they can work with technology teachers and assistants in the lab. The synergy of co-planning and co-teaching in the lab should not be underestimated. Collaboration elevates the level of thinking.

Classroom teachers are also more accountable for their use of technology when they visit the lab weekly. The technology teacher figures out quickly whether teachers are continuing to use technology in the classroom or are treating technology use as a lab-only activity. With help from the administrator, the technology teacher can determine how to support and motivate the teachers who need to grow in this area.

The following sections address various organizational tools Lenski uses to make lab and classroom use of technology easier.

Workspaces

Students have assigned desks or cubbies for their workplace tools in the classroom. It makes sense, then, that the lab, which is an extension of the classroom, should have assigned workspaces with appropriate tools as well. Interestingly, as we introduce organization tools in the lab, teachers often adopt them for their computer areas in the classroom as well. Most of these ideas can work in either place.

In the lab and classrooms, teachers often number the computers to make it easier to identify where students should work. In the lab, students can be assigned to computers by number, which not only makes finding the computer in a row of look-alikes easier, but also lends itself to an orderly dismissal from the lab. The numbers also keep all the tools for specific computers together and make it easier to recover a file if a student mistakenly saves it on the C drive rather than the server. The biggest advantage is the ability to refer to a computer number when redirecting a volunteer, who might not know students' names, to a child who needs help.

Classroom teachers have found that numbering computers makes it easier to identify any computers that need attention from the tech staff. Teachers also can differentiate for students by loading different activities on each computer and then assigning students to specific computer numbers during center time.

FIGURE 5.1 Organizing the computer workspace helps children work efficiently. Many of the practices followed in the lab have been adopted by classroom teachers to organize their classroom computer workspaces.

The numbers for many computers adhere to the fronts of small square paper holders, which are attached to the CPUs with hook and loop fasteners. The paper holders not only stand papers upright for word processing, but a small opening in the base provides a convenient pencil holder.

Because we use donated computers in the classrooms and lab, some CD players are fussy about the CDs they will play. Numbering the CDs to match the computer's number means that we can be certain the CDs at a particular computer will work in that computer. The CDs at each computer sit in a small plastic basket (also numbered) that holds about eight CDs at a time. Although we don't use specialty software often, having the CDs available at each computer simplifies management. CD baskets also hold pencils and pads of sticky notes.

Sticky notes are any teacher's friend. If students are exploring a Web site in order to develop background knowledge on a content area, any teacher, lab or classroom, can tape up chart paper with topic headings. When students learn interesting "awesome" facts, they jot the facts on sticky notes and post them on the appropriate sheets. Teachers can guide a discussion about the facts learned or have students organize them for further study. Stickies also work for editing student work, giving feedback on changes, or jotting notes to file.

Unlike the classroom, where students have private spaces, in the lab, students share their spaces with about 22 other students. A three-ring binder at each computer holds five dividers with pockets to hold papers that students may want to refer to in the lab. Although the necessity for these binders decreases every year, during some units, students may have papers they want to keep in the lab. For instance, fifth-grade students use the same formatting style for several class dictionary projects during the year. The instruction sheets can be placed in the fifth-grade binder and shared by all fifth-grade classes. Sometimes a teacher schedules her class for more than one visit in the week by taking advantage of open slots caused by other classes' field trips. Then the teacher may choose to have students keep planning sheets or original copies in the binder for later in the week.

The binders also have another use: a hard surface for writing. Sometimes a few students in a class need to work on a rough draft, solve a math problem, or take notes from a Web site. The binder can be used as if it was a clipboard.

Each student has two cards that list the student's name, user name, password, and teacher. One card is kept in the classroom in an area designated by the teacher. The other card stays in the lab. The cards for all the students assigned to a particular computer are gathered on a ring and kept in the CD basket for quick reference. Our students respect the privacy of others' computer files, or perhaps they are too busy to have time to check someone else's files, because we've never had problems with this. They often shuffle through the cards to see who sits at their computer, though.

To help non-reading students identify the important keys of the keyboard, we put tiny sticker dots on them. Using different colors for each type of key (Shift, Enter, and Tab) means that we can use the key name and the color of dot to direct students to the right keys.

Wiping down keyboards, mice and tables has become increasingly important with the recent enrollment of several students with severe allergies. Like the classrooms, the lab keeps disinfecting wipes available to clean surfaces regularly.

School practices vary related to using headphones in labs. Many schools distribute, or ask parents to provide as a school supply, individual headsets in plastic bags for each student. This addresses sanitary issues such preventing the transmission of head lice and makes students accountable if their headsets break. While working on computers, students often mindlessly twist the cords, pick at the foam, and adjust the headbands, all of which make the headsets unusable eventually. When schools can manage the distribution and storage of personal headsets, I recommend it.

Lenski has not adopted personal headsets for students, probably because no one has yet considered the current practices problematic. However, this topic will need to be broached soon as a safety issue for students with severe allergies.

Whether a school uses personal headsets or shared headsets, when possible, the Audio Out port on the computer should have a splitter to allow two sets of headphones to be attached at the same time. That way, when students complain about not hearing sound, a second person can plug into the audio to listen and determine whether the problem is the headset or the computer's volume settings or sound card. Also, if a student is having difficulty, the teacher can plug in to hear the instructions. Finally, two students can share one computer if they each have headsets.

Computer Desktops

Teachers learn quickly that a unified computer desktop (what is visible on the screen when computers are on) makes a huge difference in teaching young children. Most kindergarteners cannot read and some cannot even recognize letters, so directing them to open a program is difficult unless there is consistency in what they see.

Some schools have invested in desktop management software, which simplifies maintaining and restoring desktops. In fact, I visited one school in the neighboring district where, no matter how the students rearranged the desktops during a computer session, when they logged in the next time, Apple Remote Desktop 3 restored the standard image. Since children can inadvertently move, rename, or trash icons, such software is probably an invaluable timesaver. Any Internet search on desktop management software will bring up several options for purchasing remote management software applications such as Mac Apple Remote 3 or ME Cluster RemoteNet. Costs range from free open-source software to $450.

Those who lack such management tools, though, need to create systems for helping students develop independence.

We try not to litter the desktop so that students have fewer chances for error. All screens have icons to launch the drawing program and the Internet because students use those programs often. We also use an icon for the network so that students can easily find their individual files. The desktop has a shortcut to the mouse control so that students can change the orientation of the mouse for right- or left-handedness.

Additionally, each desktop has several folders. One, named CD Activities, holds icons to launch programs for which we use CDs. Another labeled simply Activities holds icons to launch freeware and networked programs. When students finish their work early, they are permitted to choose a program from the Activities folder. Even though the programs are all educational, students consider this a reward because they so rarely have free time on computers at school.

Another folder on the desktop is called Student Files. This holds a separate folder labeled for each kindergarten and first grade-class. We usually do not ask kindergarten and first-grade students to log onto their computers because the process takes them too long. Instead, we direct them to their class' folder inside the Student Files folder. That's where we keep templates for projects and also store finished work. In our system, students must be logged on in order to print. If we have a class of older students in the lab before kindergarten or first grade is scheduled, we ask them to log onto the network with a generic account (i.e.; username: jkjk, password: 1234) before they leave the lab. This saves the lab teachers considerable time, and older students love being helpful.

In the classroom, teachers of the youngest students copy the Student Files concept. They build one master folder with all the templates they expect to use during the year (we keep a sample on the server that they can customize). They copy that folder to the desktop as many times as they have students. Then they can rename each folder with the name of a student in the class. Students can open their folders to get the templates to complete their work. While setting it up initially takes time, it saves time in the long run.

Schedules

Schedules keep elementary schools humming. In the lab, we post three weeks' worth of schedules so that teachers in the lab can write reminders on the following week of where the lessons should pick up from the previous week or what unit/project will be introduced next. Since often two or more classes will be involved in similar projects, but at different points of completion, the notes help everyone remember where each class ended. At the end of the year, the notes are transcribed onto the technology curriculum maps to help teachers when they are planning for the following year.

Having the weekly schedule posted makes teachers aware of when the lab will be free as well. When a class on a field trip misses their lab time, another class can sign up for the slot.

In the classroom the schedules organize students, not classes. Teachers can make rotation schedules to ensure that each student gets a turn on the computers before anyone else gets a second turn. The use of a rotation list relieves the teacher of having to make daily plans for who goes first.

Expectations for Student Behavior

Because the lab extends the classroom, students follow essentially the same behavior expectations in the lab and classrooms, especially since their teachers attend lab with them. However, the combination of demonstrating mastery of curriculum while learning and practicing technology skills creates a different environment than the classroom. In the lab, students have more leeway for talking. For instance, when students are exposed to new information, we encourage them to turn and talk with a neighbor. This is particularly powerful when students are encountering new background information or studying photos and drawing conclusions.

Peer coaching is expected. Typically, students will coach peers sitting near them, although, on occasion, students may become roaming experts and help anyone who has difficulty.

Volunteers

We encourage volunteers in the lab and classrooms. Even if the volunteers have few computer skills, they can assist with class management.

At times, we ask specific parents to help in the lab, particularly if parents demonstrate unrealistic expectations for their children. Teachers have learned that these parents can be invited to assist in the lab and, while they help all children with computer skills, actually get a better picture of how their own children compare to the typical child. This is particularly striking when children are working on interactive Web sites that track correct answers versus mistakes or when children are typing paragraphs. In a lab setting, unlike a classroom, parent volunteers can see many screens at same time from any spot in the room.

Asking kindergarteners to type the numbers from 0 to 100, for instance, quickly shows which students are advanced and which are lagging. Consider using this tactic prior to parent-teacher conferences for parents who might be surprised by your assessment of their children's progress.

Because technology use extends throughout the school, many issues come up regularly. Developing a plan for addressing these issues helps teachers know what to expect.

Troubleshooting

The acquisition of reliable equipment has decreased the demand for emergency troubleshooting, but teachers occasionally experience frustration with balky technology. They use several means for solving problems.

First, teachers are encouraged to try troubleshooting on their own. Since volunteers provide technical support, teachers know that even if a computer ends up unusable, the parts will be salvageable. They can try simple fixes, such as rebooting a computer and checking plugs and switches. Some teachers enjoy the challenge, and others allow their most technically-minded students to try problem solving.

At many grade levels, one teacher often becomes the technical guru for his/her teammates, so teachers can always ask a teammate for help. In fourth and fifth grades, students also solve simple problems.

Teachers who are easily frustrated assess whether the problem needs to be fixed immediately or within a day. For immediate help, they send a student to find a technology teacher. If the solution can wait a day, teachers can either e-mail for help or write a short description of the problems on a clipboard that hangs in the mini-lab. Occasionally, teachers prefer to wait until a technology volunteer shows up after school. This is particularly true if the teacher wants to learn how to solve a specific type of problem.

Whenever possible, problems are handled as teaching moments. Often a technically-minded student or the teacher will be invited to manage the mouse during problem-solving. Although it often takes longer initially, this training pays dividends later when they can solve similar problems themselves.

Printers

In 1999, printing caused 75% of the problems in a day. The school had two printers for 600 students, and the color printer regularly failed. Teachers complained that students disappeared for 30 minutes at a time when they went to collect print jobs.

The school has invested in color laser printers and the Curriculum Innovation Team has placed them strategically around the school. Although costly, adding several identical and reliable printers has paid off in decreased frustration and improved time management for me as well as the students. Now only teachers who print confidential paperwork have individual printers.

Printing consumes cases of paper, and we used to take a ream or two from a central storage space several times a week. We have streamlined this by asking the custodian to deliver a case of paper to each networked printer. The custodian monitors the cases and replenishes them when the supply gets low.

Scanners

At first, Lenski didn't have any working scanners. Instead, we used a digital camera to take photographs of family snapshots and other pictures. Eventually, the CIT decided to invest in twelve identical, inexpensive scanners. These scanners have been placed in every third-, fourth-, and fifth-grade classroom so that each teacher has constant access for quick scanning projects. When multiple students need access to scanners, teachers can send them to neighboring classrooms. Having identical scanners decreases training needs for students and teachers. However, scanner use has continually decreased as digital cameras have become more popular.

Shared Equipment

Teachers have access to shared equipment, such as digital cameras, and portable word processors. These are generally housed in the media center and teachers sign them out. Students may also borrow portable word processors for overnight use. They must check them out at the end of the school day and return them before school begins. Using the library system to track technology has saved the tech staff countless hours of tracking equipment.

The acquisition of wireless notebook carts has added another management issue to already hectic schedules. Four teachers whose classrooms are strategically placed around the building host the carts in their classrooms. Staff members sign out the carts on sheets attached to the mobile labs. While this system means that the technology staff doesn't always know where and when the carts are being used, it has made the carts more visible and accessible to teachers. The use of an e-mail-based calendar system would also be an excellent way to track the carts.

Student Work

Teachers have different methods for handling students' finished products. In some classrooms, teachers divide their bulletin boards with a large square for each student. Students hang their works in progress on the board so that the teacher can do a visual scan to determine where students are in their projects.

FIGURE 5.2 Fourth-grade teacher Marion Honemann looks over a student's current project. Each student has a square with two clips where work in progress can hang until it is completed. Eventually, students will add these projects to their three-ring binder portfolios.

In some classrooms, students put their finished work into portfolios as a record of their year. In other classes, the teachers make books of each project. During free reading time, students can choose to read one another's work. An unexpected benefit of this model is that students sometimes catch errors weeks later and ask for permission to revise their work!

In some classes, students take their work home regularly, although many teachers have begun to keep notebook portfolios for each student.

In a few classrooms, teachers either e-mail student work to parents or post it on teacher-maintained Web sites. When the district introduces its redesigned Web site in the summer of 2006, teachers are expected to find the new Web software easier to use. If so, teachers will be more likely to post students' work on the Web site than they have been in the past.

The thoughtful use of organizational tools has saved time for all Lenski staff. Every year, we tweak the system slightly to make the management of technology more transparent to students and classroom teachers.

PART 2

Integrating Technology in the Elementary Classroom

Chapter 6

Drawing

OF THE NINE STRATEGIES THAT HAVE A POSITIVE EFFECT on student achievement (Marzano et al., 2001), drawing programs support one particularly well: non-linguistic representation. Non-linguistic representation refers to creating visuals to represent vocabulary or curricular concepts. The projects in this chapter, and in many of the following chapters, demonstrate the use of visuals to enhance students' comprehension and recollection of essential ideas.

For kindergarteners, who often think of the computer as a toy, the use of drawing programs also helps them transition to thinking of the computer as a tool. Because most kindergarteners cannot read or write, they express their ideas and individuality through pictures, so drawing can serve as the backbone of computer instruction for them. Older students enjoy using drawing programs periodically to express creativity and to demonstrate their grasp of curricular content.

The most commonly known commercial drawing software, Kid Pix, rates high among many students and teachers, but schools have other options as well. Consider taking advantage of open-source software or the free drawing programs included as part of operating systems and productivity suites.

These programs include the basic tools necessary for most projects—and the price is right. In fact, simple drawing programs may be preferable to glitzy commercial software. When software has too many options, students' creative work is often stifled. They believe that pictures created with stamps, special effects, and computer-generated objects are "better" than the drawings they create from their own imaginations. Original drawings are windows to students' thinking and are priceless treasures for parents.

Some drawing projects could be done just as easily with crayons and paper, so a teacher may question the reason for using computers for these. First, computers are an integral tool of the classroom. Just as students need to learn the motor skills involved in coloring and cutting, they need to learn to manipulate a mouse and keyboard. Even though many households have computers, in my experience, a few students every year have no experience using a mouse and, on rare occasions, may not even realize that the movement of the mouse causes the cursor to move. Additionally, the computer motivates some students in ways that a box of crayons never will.

Kindergarten students should use a drawing program at least once a month—frequent enough that they don't need much review of the tools, yet not so often that they tire of it. When primary students start the year by drawing self-portraits, teachers can assess students' self-awareness, motor skills, and familiarity with computers. Such drawings make great samples for portfolios and parent-teacher conferences as well.

Non-literate students should use drawing programs liberally so that they can demonstrate what they know about the curriculum. Older students may use drawing software less often, but drawing is an excellent way for them to express creativity and their mastery of curricular concepts as well

Kindergarten students learn how to use a few tools at a time. At the beginning, they learn the paintbrush, paint bucket (fill), color palette, and Edit...Undo. We discourage the use of the eraser because too often their immature fine motor skills lead to erasing more than they intended. A good way to demonstrate that with students is to have them make three shapes on their screens and try to erase the middle one. Invariably, they will accidentally erase the edges of the other two as well. While we don't typically do a lesson on fixing mistakes, showing students alternatives to erasing may be worthwhile. For instance, students could color a mistake the same color as the background, draw over their mistakes, or, in extreme cases, start over.

Introducing additional tools depends on the teacher's assessment of a students' readiness, but in every class, a few adventurous and curious students experiment with tools on their own and they spread the knowledge to their neighbors. Celebrate this initiative as evidence that students are ready for more.

RESOURCES

Popular Drawing Programs

Kid Pix Deluxe 4 by Broderbund (www.broderbund.com): An easy-to-use and popular program for home or school; many options such as stamps, slide shows, complex tools. Priced around $20 per computer for single education copies; about $900 for 50-computer network license.

Tux Paint (www.tuxpaint.org): Similar to Kid Pix, Tux Paint offers glitzy tools and options but without the price tag. As open-source software, the program is continually being updated and can be downloaded at no cost. The biggest disadvantage to Tux Paint is the limitation on saving files. Tux Paint saves all pictures within the program itself.

Microsoft Paint: Found in Accessories as part of the Windows operating system, Paint does not cost extra. This program has basic drawing tools only. The lack of stamps and special effects means that students must rely on their own drawing skills when they create pictures. Text can be added to pictures, but cannot be reactivated for editing. Students can insert copied clip art and pictures that have been first inserted in other applications.

AppleWorks Draw: Part of the AppleWorks software package (no additional licensing fee), Draw is more robust and versatile than Microsoft Paint, but is still basic. Text is editable and clip art provided. The advantage to AppleWorks is that drawing capability is included within the productivity suite, so that students can create drawings within any document, spreadsheet, or presentation under construction.

Students' use of drawing programs becomes more sophisticated over time. First graders draw the water cycle; third graders illustrate their favorite books, and fifth graders overlay drawing onto photographs. Teachers use drawing projects to assess students' understanding of concepts. Looking at students' drawings of a habitat or the life cycle of a butterfly shows how well the students grasped science concepts. Differentiation is easy: students with advanced skills typically add details that others have missed, and struggling students create simplified products.

To satisfy students' curiosity about what classmates have drawn, a teacher can conduct gallery walks. During gallery walks, students stroll through the room as though they were visiting an art show. Gallery walks work with any projects and all age groups. Students enjoy showing off their work and seeing how their classmates have interpreted an assignment.

Lenski spends a lot on printer ink. If your budget won't allow such extravagance, students' artwork can be handled other ways. Explore whether you can e-mail the pictures home or import them into presentation software for a slide show. At the end of the year, a slide show of each student's work can be burned on a CD or e-mailed to parents. As long as the projects don't identify individual students by their whole names and you have signed releases from parents, work can be posted to a class Web site as well. During parent teacher conferences, you can even set up continuous loop slide shows of student work.

Ideas for Drawing Projects

The following project descriptions often refer to making a template. How a school implements this will depend on the school's set-up. Although the Word template implies a document that cannot be changed, we use it to describe any pre-formatted document that students will use as a base for their work. At Lenski, we load the original on the server and copy it to a shared folder where students can access it and save a copy in their own folders. Some schools have management software that sends documents to every computer simultaneously. Other schools may have different systems. In this book, the Word template simply means a teacher-created document that looks the same for every student.

Typically, kindergarteners get two opportunities to create each picture. The first week, they make practice pictures, which the teachers often save in case a student is absent the following week. Then students do a gallery walk. This lets them collect additional ideas for their final picture the following week and satisfies their desire to share their work with others. The second week, students come into the lab with a clear idea of what they want to draw and, usually, the final pictures have more detail.

Depending on students' ages, they will need differing amounts of time to complete their drawings. Generally, young students complete pictures within twenty minutes, although a few students will require longer, either because they use meticulous detail or because they get off to a slow start. Given too much time, primary students will often scribble on or color over their drawings to the extent that their pictures will lose their charm and meaning.

Intermediate students (Grades 3–5) need at least half an hour to complete a picture, and perfectionists will take even longer. For this reason, teachers need to have additional activities such as interactive Web sites or skill software for the early finishers. The enticement of another activity causes the slowest students to speed up in order not to miss out.

The following drawing integration ideas can be adapted to align with other curricular targets or grade levels. Better yet, they may spur your own creativity.

Hundreds Day Chart (K–1)

Create a template with ten empty squares of various sizes and load it on each computer. Instruct students to place ten colored shapes in each box. Students who finish early can add labels that count by 10s.

FIGURE 6.1 Kindergarten teacher Diane Flagg reviews the expectations for the Hundreds Day Chart during the second computer session of the project.

Following Directions (K–1)

Draw or download a coloring book-style picture with several large areas for painting. Read a simple color rhyme (write your own) to instruct students what to color each section. For example, if you used a picture from *The Three Little Pigs*, one rhyme could be: "My house is sturdy, the third pig said. Find his house and paint it _____." Students guess "red" and paint the brick house. A gallery walk after this project will reveal that even though students use the same colors, the hues they choose will make their pictures look different.

Glyph (K–1)

Create a template of a basic featureless snowman (or pumpkin face, scarecrow, etc.) for students to color. Give students instructions to follow as they personalize the picture. Example: Add one button for every person who lives in your house; make the eyes the same color as your own eyes, add a hat feather for each pet you have. Again, students will enjoy a gallery walk to see the finished pictures.

Illustrations (K–5)

Students can demonstrate their understanding of content through their drawings. After completing research, students can create illustrations to accompany their reports. Students also illustrate their favorites: a book, memory of a grandparent, part of the school day, teacher, or activity. All these can be added to slide shows, word processing, or simply printed as is.

Some students use drawings to illustrate poems. After a unit on poetry, students use pictures to capture the figurative language and main idea of one or more of the poems.

For a charity project, students draw holiday illustrations and import them into a desktop publishing program as the front of a greeting card. When the drawings are reduced to fit the cards, they look intricately detailed.

Portraits (K–5)

At any grade level, self-portraits develop a sense of community within a classroom. The rough drawings produced by primary students sometimes give insight to what they consider distinctive about themselves. Intermediate students can use their self-portraits to illustrate original poems about themselves, for a 'Who Am I?' riddle, or as part of a collage of original art and clip art.

During a study of family and community life, kindergarteners often demonstrate their understanding of the unit by drawing a family portrait or a picture of a community helper such as a police officer, firefighter, medical worker, etc.

FIGURE 6.2 Lindsey, a fifth grader, used this self-portrait to illustrate a biographic poem. Fifth-grade portraits are often amazingly recognizable.

Half-pages (K–2)

Some lessons lend themselves to half, rather than whole, pages. For Earth Day, students draw how the world will look if we don't care for it and how it will look if we do take care. After learning about another period in history, a student might illustrate the difference between life then and now. Students can draw pictures of objects belonging in two different geometric shape categories. A picture in which a student draws short vowel sound objects on one side and long vowel sound objects on another helps a teacher assess whether the student hears vowels correctly. The page may be divided horizontally or vertically, depending on the topic.

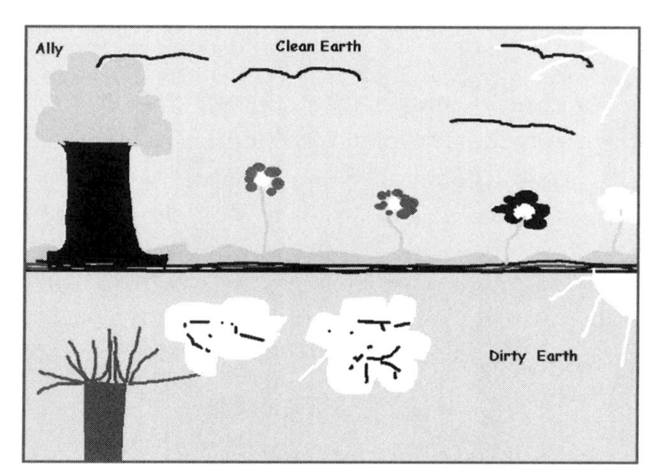

FIGURE 6.3 On Earth Day, first-grader Ally drew the contrast between a cared-for Earth and a polluted one.

Four Squares (K–5)

Young students sometimes find it challenging to fill an entire page. Consider the many ways of using a page divided into four sections. For instance, after a classroom teacher reads a book about favorite things, students draw four favorite things. These pictures become the topics for four journal writing entries.

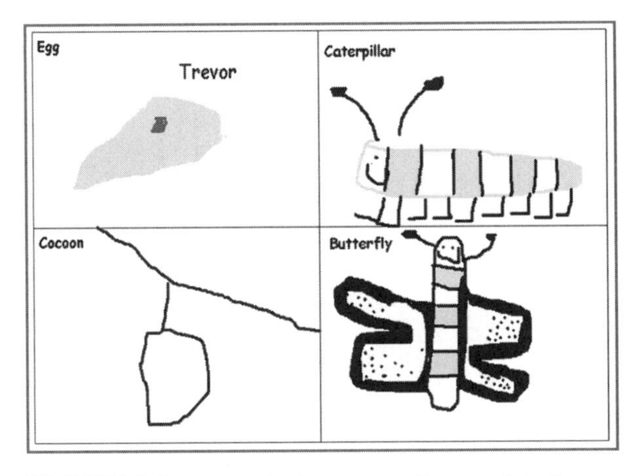

FIGURE 6.4 Trevor, a kindergartener, illustrated the four stages of a butterfly's life as a demonstration of what he had learned in the classroom.

During insect studies, students learn about four insects (butterfly, praying mantis, bee, and ladybug) through Web sites. Their four squares are labeled with these insect names. The teacher reads a rhyme and students draw a picture of the answer in the right square. They try to include the habitat for the insects as well, which can lead to charmingly different pictures. One student, who found drawing difficult, colored his praying mantis square with a green scribble and two antennae. He said the praying mantis was camouflaged!

Students can draw four examples of anything: types of volcanoes, weather, mammals, seasons, rocks, and so forth. For some students the physical act of drawing makes the information more memorable, and the use of the computer is motivating.

Variation: The page can be divided into as many parts as a teacher needs. One teacher divided the three sections for students to draw the beginning, middle, and end of a short story.

Four-step Processes (K–5)

After students have studied the water cycle, food chains, or any other process with four steps, they can illustrate what they know. Use a template with the screen divided into four squares. Add arrows to show the cycle. Students draw the steps of the process and label each part. For the water cycle, students may want to create a water drop character and name it. That way they can follow their droplet characters through the cycle.

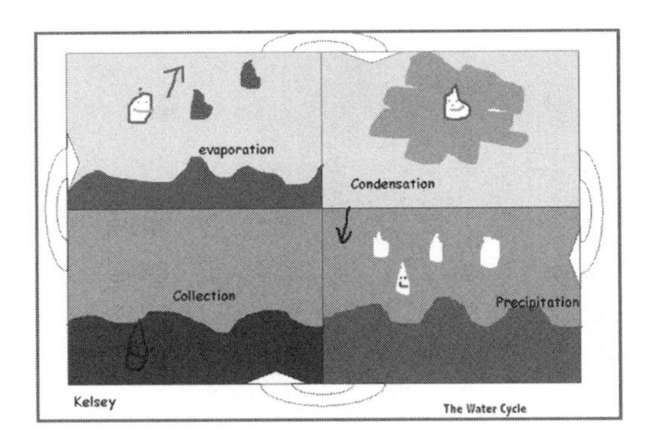

FIGURE 6.5 First-grader Kelsey chose to start the water cycle with evaporation and created a water droplet to follow through the process.

Riddles (1–5)

Students can draw an object and write a riddle about it for their classmates to guess. For example, after a unit on nutrition, students draw a nutritious food and write a three-clue riddle. Students can draw a famous person in history (perhaps the person about whom they read a biography), a planet, or a mammal.

Visual Vocabulary (1–5)

Teachers use visual vocabulary to strengthen students' recall in content areas. During unit studies of insects, mammals, and amphibians, first graders frequently choose creatures to draw and label. The teacher provides a word chart so that students can label as many parts as they remember.

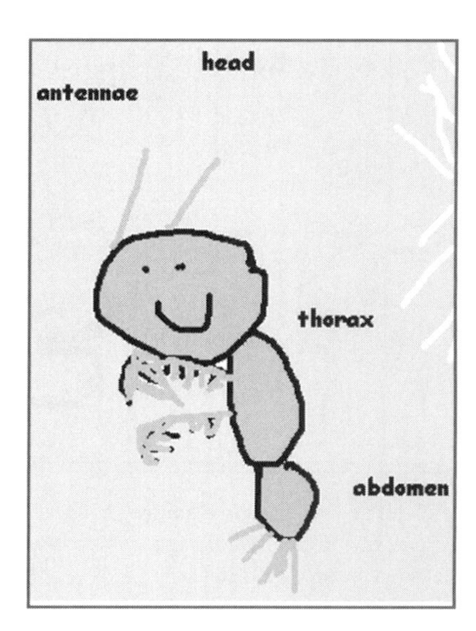

FIGURE 6.6 Andrew, a first grader, demonstrated that he understood the body sections of an insect.

Geography lends itself to non-linguistic representation as well. One teacher assigns each student a geography term to illustrate. Students draw visuals that illustrate the terms and add the words and definitions. Once printed, these are gathered into a notebook for the classroom library. Another teacher has students illustrate six math terms on a page divided into six squares. Students create pictures that match the terms and label them.

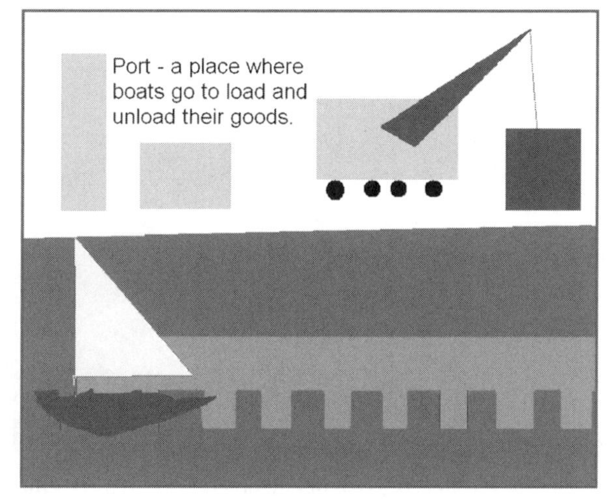

FIGURE 6.7 Sam and Jake collaborated on a picture to explain the word "port," which is an unfamiliar term to many students in landlocked Colorado.

Visual representations are particularly effective for content-related terms. Students may also illustrate idioms, daily or weekly vocabulary words, or abstract values such as liberty and hope.

Growth Processes (2-4)

When students have studied plants, they can create a series of pictures in which the plant goes through its growth cycle. The first picture takes the longest because they need to create a background for their plant, draw the seed underground, and label it. They save this picture as "Seed." They then save the same picture, using Save As and naming it "Seedling." On the second picture, they add the sprouting of the seed to just above ground and label it. They save this picture and then Save As "Leaves." In this next picture they add leaves to the seedling and label them. After they save the picture, they once again use Save As for the next picture. Continue this process until the plant has bloomed. Import the pictures into a slide show and set the slides to advance automatically every three seconds. When the slide show runs, the plants seem to grow.

FIGURE 6.8 As a culminating activity for a unit on plants, Maria created a series of pictures showing the plant growth cycle. She then inserted them into presentation software to make a slide show to show the plant "growing."

Tessellations (2–5)

To make a tessellation, students first draw a colored square or rectangle. Using the selection tool, they cut the tessellation with a jagged line. Their line starts on the top side, moves through the figure vertically without overlapping, goes out the bottom of the figure, and loops all the way around half of the figure to the beginning point. This selects a portion of the figure which can be dragged to the other side of the original figure. The sides that meet will be straight lines that can match up exactly and make a figure with jagged edges.

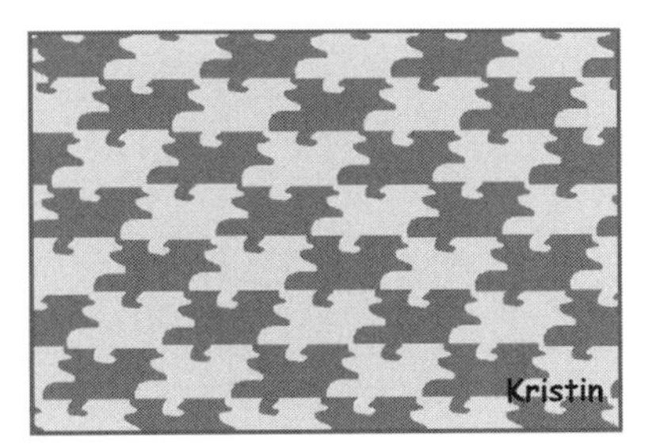

FIGURE 6.9 Kristin's second-grade class completed tessellations near the end of the school year. For the first experience, everyone worked together, but several students made multiple samples, adding complexity as they experimented.

Students repeat the process cutting through the figure horizontally. They drag the cut-out to the bottom of the figure so that the figure now has jagged edges on all sides.

Select the entire figure, copy it, and paste it on another part of the page. Color the pasted figure a different color. Then drag it next to the first figure so that both fit side-by-side perfectly as a tessellation. Select the paired figures and copy them. Paste repeatedly to fill the entire page. Once students master this technique, they make more and more complex tessellations and create incredible mosaic artwork.

Original Symbols (4–5)

When students study state history, they learn the symbols included on the state seal and flag. They then can create their own seals, flags, or even patches like astronaut patches. Students have discovered that, even with a basic drawing program, they can import clip art and incorporate it into their original drawings.

FIGURE 6.10 Four fourth graders, Jason, Peter, Pierce, and Zach, collaborated on an astronaut patch, which combined original art with WordArt, for their Space Day t-shirts.

Drawing programs offer a wide variety of educational opportunities in the elementary school. They engage students in creatively expressing what they've learned about content and allow for the range of abilities within a classroom. Because the use of drawing programs is easy to master and most of these projects can be completed quickly, teachers will find them appropriate for classroom computers as well as lab experiences.

Clip Art in Microsoft Paint

While the other drawing programs have clip art embedded, Microsoft Paint offers no standard option for adding clip art. However, with a little extra effort, you can mix clip art, photos, and WordArt with your original drawings in Microsoft Paint, as I demonstrated in the Colorado sample below. You will need to open an Office application such as Word or PowerPoint in addition to the Paint program. Insert the clip art, photo, or WordArt into the Office application. For instance, in the picture below, I inserted a clip art picture of a sun into a Word document. I then copied it and pasted it into Paint. I used the fill bucket to re-color the image and the selection tool to move it into position.

After I drew and colored the mountain backdrop, I inserted clip art of columbine, Colorado's state flower, into the Word document. I resized, copied, and pasted the flowers into the Paint picture. Pasted items come into Paint as selected items in the upper left hand corner, so I left the sky uncolored until the end. While the flowers were in the upper corner and selected, I used several options. On the top toolbar, I selected Image...Rotate/Flip to rotate some of the images horizontally. Along the side toolbar I selected the last box with colored images in it, which made the area around the clip art invisible. I could then drag the flowers to set them in the picture. When the flowers were set, I painted the sky. Finally, I used WordArt in Word to add the word Colorado, copied the text, and pasted it into my picture.

FIGURE 6.11 Clip art sun used in larger picture.

FIGURE 6.12 Drawn in Microsoft Paint, this picture combines clip art and WordArt with an original drawing.

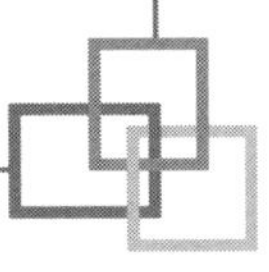

LESSON PLAN

Kindergarten, The Five Senses

TEACHERS(S):	COLLABORATIVE PARTNER(S):
Kindergarten	Technology Teacher
CURRICULAR AREA(S):	CONTENT TARGET(S):
Science	Understanding senses
Writing	Best-guess spelling

STANDARDS ADDRESSED:

National Science Content Standards K–4:

C. Understanding the characteristics of organisms

National Language Arts Standards:

4. Communicating ideas to various audiences

ISTE National Technology Standards for Students:

2. Using productivity tools to enhance learning, promote creativity, and produce creative works

FINAL PRODUCT:

- Students will create a five-part drawing that visually represents how the five senses are used. Students will write in their daily journals about each sense.

NECESSARY SKILLS (CONTENT, TECHNOLOGY, INFORMATION LITERACY):

Content:

- Knowledge of the five senses; knowledge of writing conventions such as left-to-right lettering; letter sounds for approximate spelling

Technology:

- Using a drawing program to complete a template; navigating an Internet site; using the class document camera

TIMELINE:

DATES	PERSON RESPONSIBLE:	ACTIVITY:
WEEK 1	Classroom Teacher	Introduce five senses through literature, hands-on experiments, rhythm poems, and songs. Activity ideas can be found at the Southwest Educational Development Laboratory (www.sedl.org/scimath/pasopartners/senses/welcome.html). Five students per day bring a show-and-tell related to that day's sense; use the document camera to share the items with the class. Students write about one sense a day in their daily journals.
	Technology Teacher	Demonstrate the five senses template and review the drawing tools.
	Both Teachers	Students draw an example of how they use each sense in daily life.
WEEK 2	Classroom Teacher	Using projector, teacher and students visit Sesame Street's Your Amazing Body Web site (www.sesameworkshop.org/sesamestreet/games/flash.php?contentId=108866) to practice identifying how the senses work. Students work in pairs at the classroom computers on the Sesame Street Web site.
	Both Teachers	In the lab, students complete their senses drawings, label the items, and print.

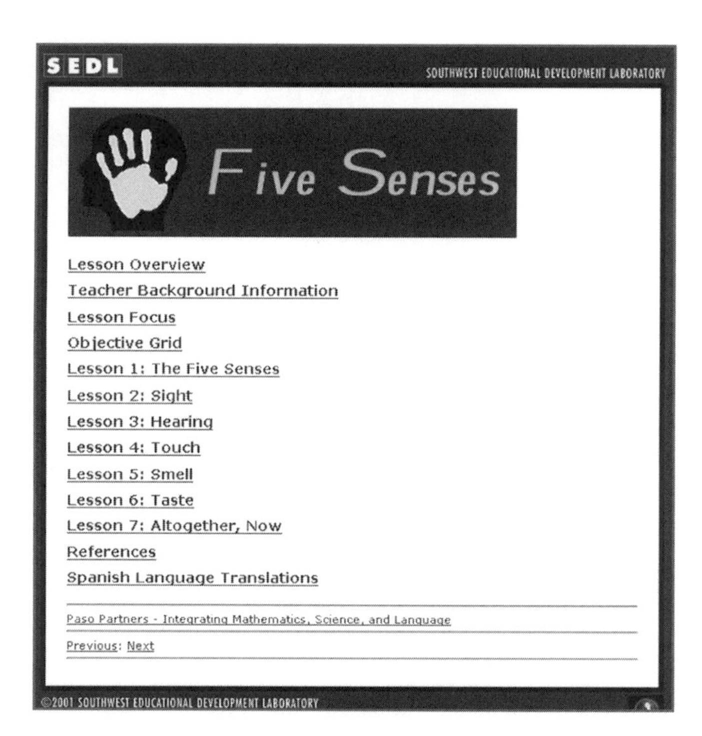

FIGURE 6.13 The Southwest Educational Development Laboratory has published a unit on the five senses that includes literature, art, and science ideas for the classroom teacher.

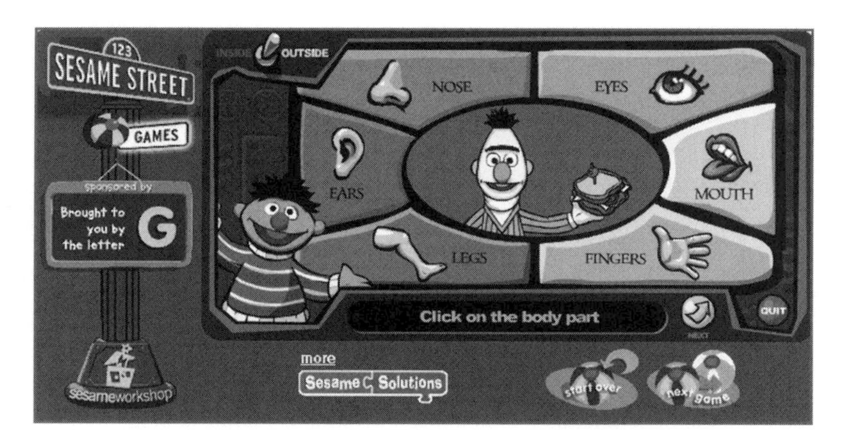

FIGURE 6.14 In this interactive module from Sesame Street, Ernie narrates so students receive oral support. The combination of oral support, pictures, and words ensures that students can be successful.

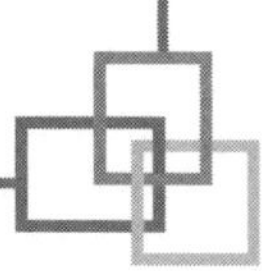

What Bugs Me

Out of all the things that bug me, boys, traffic, and homework bug me the most. To begin, boys bug me so much. They are very weird and they act gross. They spit, drool, and kiss. In addition, traffic can be so annoying. It makes you late for things that you need to be at. The cars are honking and polluting air, too. Finally, homework ruins your playtime. It's boring and sometimes is hard. When you're watching a TV show your parents say, "Time to do your homework," and then they turn off the TV. In retrospect, boys, traffic, and homework bug me the most.

By Drew

Chapter 7

Word Processing

IN MANY CASES, WORD PROCESSING IS COMPLETELY INTERCHANGEABLE with pencil and paper. After all, text is text, whether a student writes by hand or types. But sometimes word processing has advantages over handwriting.

Keyboarding gives instant feedback to students about spelling errors and provides options for corrections. Poor spellers can get so bogged down looking for errors that they lose focus on their main goal, communicating ideas. Even though spell checking misses some errors, it assists students in identifying and correcting a majority of their mistakes.

With proper instruction, students can learn to use the built-in thesaurus to spice up their writing. For example, when the word "have" pops up in every sentence, they can look for more specific words to substitute. The thesaurus helps them recognize the nuances of words and provides alternatives to the overused words in their writing.

Word processing eases the editing process as well. Students can reorganize their text by moving words, lines, and paragraphs, rather than starting over. They can insert new details or substitute vibrant language more easily into typed text than into a handwritten piece.

Best of all, typed text levels the field for evaluating writing. When every piece of writing has the same legibility, a teacher, parent, or student can focus on the words and ideas without the bias that handwriting, particularly poor handwriting, introduces. In hand- written text, a paper with precisely formed letters and straight margins will tend to be viewed as better writing than a paper with a barely legible scrawl and messy corrections. The tidier paper suggests more orderly thinking, whether true or not. Typed text removes this bias.

On the other hand, word processing can *introduce* bias to text evaluation. When students have permission to embellish their text with fancy features, such as color, pictures, and font styles, the artistry of their presentation can also prejudice a reader to overlook content in favor of presentation. A reader's assessment of writing must always focus on the words.

Word processing covers more than just typing words, though, because of the many built-in features that enhance text. The timing of a student's introduction to particular skills will depend on what purposes their teachers provide for using the techniques. At Lenski, kindergarten and first-grade students typically type only key words or simple sentences, although, by mid-first grade, a teacher may have the students complete framed paragraphs or type a series of three to four sentences that have been written and edited in class.

Second graders "fancy up" their words with text options such as colored text, clip art, page borders, and WordArt. At each successive grade level, students add design features, many of which they discover on their own and teach through peer coaching.

Depending on the projects, intermediate students may learn to set tabs, insert tables and graphs, add shapes such as speech bubbles, use highlighters, set up columns, change bullet styles, or add headers and footers. They use the spell checker and thesaurus. They find and replace text, insert page breaks, and change the page margins.

Perhaps some of these skills will be obsolete by the time elementary students reach adulthood. In the past twenty years, word processing has become more, rather than less, powerful. Because we cannot predict how word processing will change, we teach students the vocabulary and skills of current word processing programs. Once students learn the tools of today's word processors, they can adapt to changing technology.

On Keyboarding

In order to use traditional word processing, students must be able to type. People disagree about when and how to teach keyboarding. Some teachers address keyboard awareness beginning in kindergarten. With yarn, they separate the keyboard in half and teach students to use the left and right hands on the appropriate sides of the keyboard. Formal instruction concerning home row position and proper fingering at

Keyboarding Research

The Utah State Office of Education hosts a Web site with resources for K–12 schools related to keyboarding (www.usoe.k12.ut.us/ate/keyboarding/key.htm).

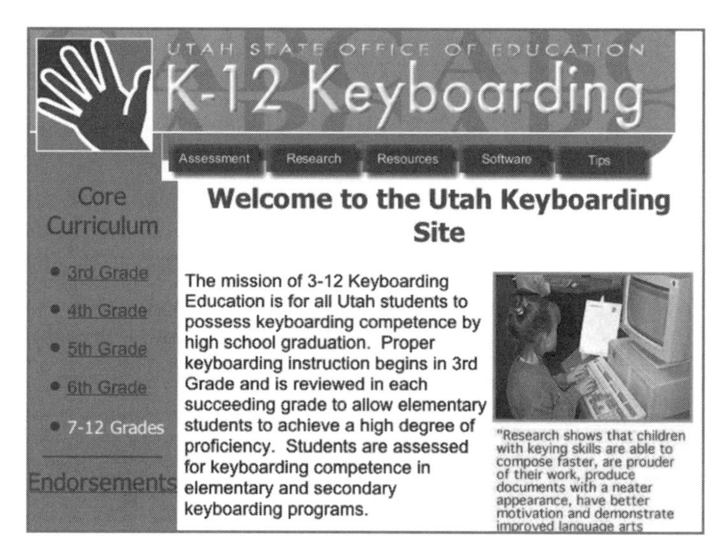

FIGURE 7.1 This site, developed by the Utah State Office of Education, has links for grades 3–12 core curriculum along the left side. Across the top in blue boxes are additional resources for teachers.

Across the top of the site are sections on assessment, research, resources, software, and tips. The research button has links to two articles that address the conflicting arguments about when to start keyboarding instruction:

"Typewriting/Keyboarding Instruction in Elementary Schools" by Lloyd W. Bartholome, www.usoe.k12.ut.us/ate/keyboarding/Articles/Bartholome.htm

"Who Should Teach Keyboarding and When Should It Be Taught?" by Margaret J. Erthal, www.usoe.k12.ut.us/ate/keyboarding/Articles/Whowhen.htm

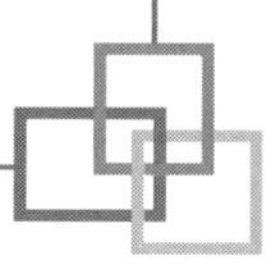

those schools often begins in second or third grade. Others recommend waiting until fourth grade when students have more coordination and larger hands.

Several high school teens, whose first formal keyboarding instruction came in middle school, have told me that they didn't become proficient touch-typists until they started Instant Messaging and blogging. When they had authentic reasons to type quickly, they mastered touch-typing.

At Lenski, because classroom teachers take responsibility for how computers are used in the classroom and the lab, the commitment to keyboarding instruction varies greatly from teacher to teacher. In the lab, students learn home row placement and proper fingering beginning in kindergarten, but teachers are so driven to complete computer-based projects with their students that they rarely devote lab time for typing practice. In late second and early third grades, we carve some time to teach letter awareness, such as the first fifteen minutes of class for a month or so, but we depend on regular production of word-processed documents to give students practice. All classrooms have portable word processors with keyboarding software so that teachers can assign keyboarding homework.

We also encourage parents to take responsibility for helping their students improve their keyboarding skills. We once had a young student whose typing left everyone behind. His parents required him to practice keyboarding for 10 minutes to earn an hour of computer games or TV. Since he loved computer games, he had practiced keyboarding daily for 10–30 minutes. Such family partnerships can benefit students and teachers.

At Lenski, our philosophy about teaching keyboarding has changed over time. We once worried that, even by second grade, many students had developed bad typing habits. We struggled to balance teaching proper keyboarding and meeting teachers' needs to have students work on computer-based projects. In a school where the teachers drive technology lessons, we realized that only when a teacher felt hampered by students' lack of keyboarding skills would he/she devote lab time to practice. Some teachers focus on keyboarding skills and some teachers don't.

Additionally, we considered that adults are rarely evaluated on their ability to touch-type. Yes, touch-typists complete their work faster. Yes, touch-typing can capture ideas more quickly than handwriting can. However, many adults have never learned to type properly, yet they successfully produce the documents they need for business and no one can tell whether they used one finger or ten. Knowing that typing is a convenient but not essential skill has caused us to relax. We introduce proper fingering and encourage students to practice, but we never evaluate their typing progress. Since students use word processing to do their schoolwork, they often find it worthwhile to learn touch-typing.

Even though we expect students to use word processing, we rarely ask them to compose at the keyboard prior to fourth grade. Through third grade, students typically write on sentence strips so that they can reorganize and edit their work before they sit down at a computer. At the computer, then, they transpose from written to typed text. This is an additional opportunity to edit, revise, and embellish.

The following ideas represent common uses of word processing. Chapter 8 will discuss using technology tools within a word processing program to improve writing.

RESOURCES

Keyboarding Resources

Keyboard Success Curriculum Kit by Ann Fidanque, Sam Miller, Mary K. Smith, and Abigail Sullivan. This kit includes a teacher's guide, student flipbook, and wall poster to be used in direct keyboarding instruction. Published by the International Society for Technology in Education (www.iste.org) and suitable for students and teachers in grades 3–9, the entire kit or individual parts cost less than $50.

Dance Mat Typing (www.bbc.co.uk/schools/typing/): This British typing site is divided into four levels, each with three sections. The online keyboarding instruction module is aimed for students ages 7–11. The site introduces home row and then gradually adds letters with practice using letter sequences and words. Worksheets are provided to reinforce the online lessons. The graphics and audio will entertain students while they learn. Of all the online typing sites I found, this was by far the most engaging.

Tux Type (http://tuxtype.sourceforge.net): This free, open-source typing program engages students either typing letters on fish for Tux the Penguin to eat or on comets for Tux to zap. Best used after students have learned finger and letter placement, the program has many levels and speeds. Tux Type can be downloaded for Windows, Mac, or Linux. We encourage families to download Tux Type for at-home keyboarding practice.

Learn2Type for Schools (www.learn2type.com/schools/whatis.cfm): This free online typing program allows teachers to enroll students and monitor their progress through a teacher console. Lessons available for K–12. There are some ads on the kids' pages unless a school buys the no-ads option.

Touch-Typing (http://sense-lang.org/typing/): This no-frills site lets you learn online or download a program at no cost. Whether practiced online or downloaded, this software introduces only two letters at a time and gives lengthy practice for each skill. Probably more appropriate for older students who are eager to learn touch-typing and don't need engaging animation.

NimbleFingers (www.nimblefingers.com/p_prog.htm): The trial version of NimbleFingers is free and works well. The advantage to this program is that it gives feedback on typing speed, number of errors, and adjusted speed. Individual and site licenses are available at prices similar to other commercial software programs. Licenses give you the option of adding and customizing exercises.

Find the Letter (www.freeWebs.com/weddell/findtheletter.html): This practice site is only for students after they have mastered the placement of all letters of the alphabet. Letters fall from the sky and the students try to type as many as possible before they hit the ground.

NOTE: The Utah Office of Education lists, rates, and provides links for many commercial keyboarding software packages on its Web site at www.usoe.k12.ut.us/ate/keyboarding/key.htm.

Hundreds Chart (K–1)

Students can use a table in a word processing program to type number charts. The charts may be used to assess students' number awareness, create a reference tool for math class, or demonstrate patterns in math.

To make a template, create a table that is ten columns wide and ten or eleven rows long. The number of rows depends on whether the zero sits at the end of the top row (eleven rows) or at the beginning of a row (ten rows) Set the font size to about 20 and center the text. Make the gridlines visible so that the table becomes a printable grid.

The reason for using word processing rather than a spreadsheet has to do with the ease of moving through a table. Students use the Tab key to proceed across the grid. When the Tab hits the end of the table in word processing, the cursor will move to the beginning of the next row. In a spreadsheet, students have to remember to press return at the end of the row, or the cursor will continue to make a very long row. In word processing, when students finish the final row, Tab will place another row at the bottom, so the rows will continue to be the same size and font. Students can then focus on their numbers and not on formatting issues.

The template needs to provide some numbers filled in as a model for students. Generally at Lenski, we type in the first eleven numbers. With the class, we model adding two more numbers before we release the students to work independently. If students are typing their charts in the lab, then adults circulate to help the strugglers and to catch mistakes before students get too far along. In a classroom, the teachers send students to work on the computers and ask them to type as many numbers as they can. The final product is a true assessment of what students know about their numbers and numeric order.

The table can be color-coded by rows, or teachers could color-code by columns instead so that students see the patterns of the ones place value in two- and three-digit numbers.

As students get older, the chart can be a way to show them the patterns made in skip counting. If students are skip-counting by two's, for instance, we teach them to type the first number, Tab and whisper the second number, Tab and type the next number. This process of Tab and whisper, Tab and type involves students visually, aurally, and experientially in developing the pattern of skip-counting. The grid ends up with blanks for the skipped numbers so students can concretely see the abstract concept of skip-counting. If the grid has also been color-coded by columns instead of rows, students can see the patterns even more clearly.

Field Trip Reports (1–5)

At any grade level, field trips give students reasons to word process. If teachers choose traditional paragraphs, students can practice their writing skills (organization, use of details, catchy beginnings, etc.) in their reports about what they learned. The addition of digital photos taken during the field trip adds realism to the report. Best of all, the finished products become public relations tools because they show parents the value of the field trips. For students who may not have access to digital photos, drawings of what they saw on the trip serve just as well.

Research Reports (1–5)

When students complete research on a science or social studies topic, they need a final product to demonstrate their work. Sometimes the final product is a report. Similar to field trip reports, research papers may be one or more paragraphs with photos or drawings, depending on the age and ability of the student.

During research, students create a question, investigate the topic, and take notes. They then write one or more paragraphs that pose and answer their question. These paragraphs are finally typed on the computer and printed.

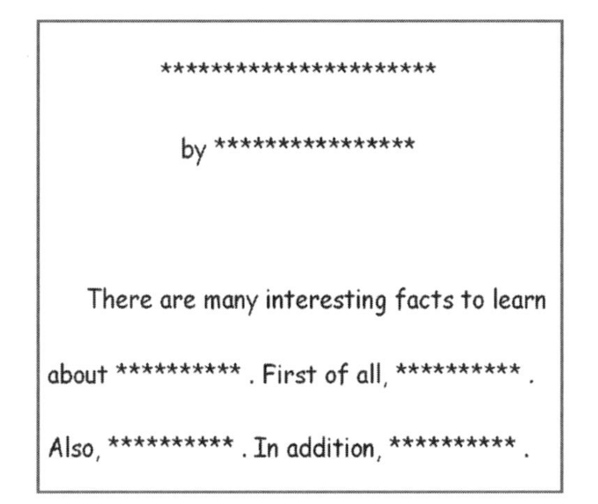

FIGURE 7.2 This framed paragraph lets first graders type their research facts without feeling overwhelmed by a blank screen. Students double-click on the stars and type their words to finish the sentences.

In the first and second grades, where students lack the keyboarding skills to be quick, they will often open a framed paragraph template where the sentence beginnings are provided and they finish the sentences with details about their research subjects.

While research reports can follow the traditional form, students may also be encouraged to write imaginative reports. For example, a report after researching an animal may take the form of a journal written by the animal in which the animal talks about its home, family, and favorite food. Students write reports on the Civil War from the viewpoint of a slave, a Rebel soldier, or a farm wife whose husband is at war. Students even use other programs to create projects such as brochures, storybooks, slide shows, or picture books.

Poetry (1–5)

Many students love to write and illustrate original poems. Consider having students create books of their own poetry as a gift for a parent. Haikus or other short poems are manageable for first graders. Older students may type longer collections of poems. One third-grade teacher creates a calendar illustrated with student poetry as a holiday gift for parents. Students write and type poems about the seasons, and she chooses five or six for each page of the calendar. At the culmination of a fourth-grade poetry unit, students create poetry books for Mother's Day.

FIGURE 7.3 Third-grader Natalie's poem about a swan creates an image with words that is enhanced by the clip art in the background.

ABC Reports (2–5)

During a staff development on best practices in literacy, Lenski teachers learned about using ABC formats to encourage students to write about what they've learned. The teachers find different ways to use the ABC concept, including field trip reports and summaries of key topics in science and social studies units such as habitats, the respiratory system, and immigration. Some students produce their ABC reports in word-processing programs.

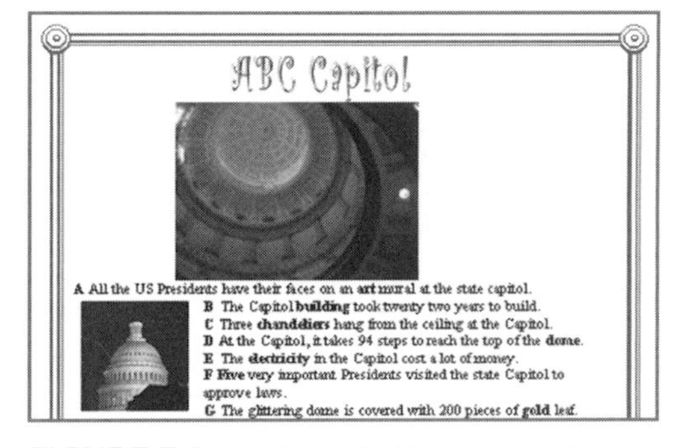

FIGURE 7.4 Fourth-grader Hannah turned her notes from the field trip to the Colorado State Capitol into an ABC report.

While some fourth-grade classes write traditional field trip reports after their trip to the Colorado Capitol building, others create ABC reports from their notes.

Conventions of Text (2–5)

One of the best ways to get students to pay attention to the conventions of nonfiction text is to ask them to follow the conventions in their own work. Students can add glossaries, captions, tables of contents, and even sidebars to their work on the computer. Lenski students have been adding hand-written tables of contents to science notebooks and research notebooks for several years, so it has been a natural extension to add the same convention to some technology-based projects.

Practice Paragraphs (2–5)

Sometimes teachers simply want students to use the computer to type a practice paragraph. The students may be focusing on a specific skill, such as grabber openings, description, or adding details, or the teachers may just be so delighted with students' responses to a writing prompt that they want others to see their students' work. In these cases, after the students have written and edited paragraphs in the classroom, they type their work. Then the teacher has a choice about whether to work with the text to improve writing (see chapter 8) or to allow students to embellish the page and print. Hanging such work in the hallway or collecting the work in portfolios can be excellent ways to document students' growth as writers.

Fiction (2–5)

Students can use word processing software to embellish fiction, whether it is a short story or a longer book for a publishing center. One second-grade teacher has her students combine clip art pictures to illustrate their stories. Another teacher asks students to draw illustrations in a painting program and import them. Reluctant writers often write longer and more complex stories when they know their typed and illustrated work will be displayed in a hallway or placed in portfolios.

Virtual E-mail (3–5)

E-mail has become a common 21st century communications tool so students need to understand its format and etiquette. Some teachers set up e-mail accounts and monitor them so that students can communicate through an intranet or the Internet.

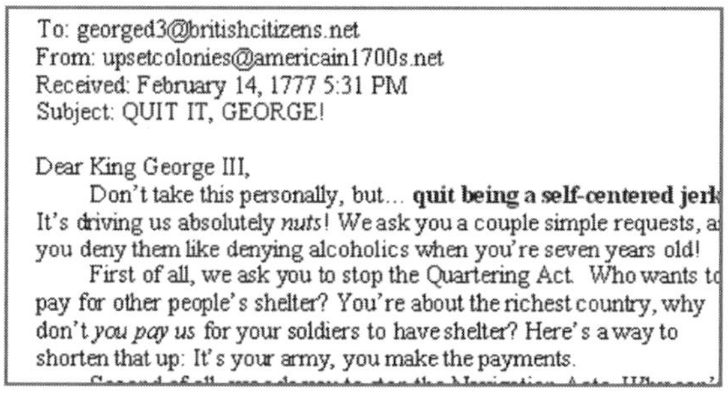

To: georged3@britishcitizens.net
From: upsetcolonies@americain1700s.net
Received: February 14, 1777 5:31 PM
Subject: QUIT IT, GEORGE!

Dear King George III,
Don't take this personally, but… **quit being a self-centered jerk**
It's driving us absolutely *nuts*! We ask you a couple simple requests, a
you deny them like denying alcoholics when you're seven years old!
First of all, we ask you to stop the Quartering Act. Who wants to
pay for other people's shelter? You're about the richest country, why
don't *you pay us* for your soldiers to have shelter? Here's a way to
shorten that up: It's your army, you make the payments.

FIGURE 7.5 This virtual e-mail by fifth-graders Andrew and Graham highlights colonial concerns prior to the American Revolution. It also opens the door for a teacher to talk about audience and tone.

Virtual e-mail can be a fun way to get students to demonstrate what they understand about a content area. Students can collaborate to write virtual e-mails to historic figures such as government leaders or famous inventors. Such role-playing causes students to think about tone, organization, and word choice. If students role-play to respond to one another's e-mails, the correspondence could lend insight to multiple perspectives around historic events.

Poetry Study (3–5)

In our computer lab, students study figurative language through a poetry unit. As a large group, students read and discuss the central ideas of 5–8 poems projected onto a large screen. Then students divide into teams to look for figurative language in each of the poems. Typically, each group works with two adjacent computers. On one computer monitor they display a page of figurative language definitions and examples. On the other screen is the poem they've been assigned. They use highlighting to mark examples of figurative language and then present their findings to the class.

Story Elements (3–5)

Word processing can be used creatively to teach the elements of fiction, such as dialogue and story elements. To teach dialogue, a fifth-grade teacher provides several single-frame cartoons or news photographs with two characters. Students pair up to write the dialogue between the characters. Each student becomes one of the characters in the picture and writes that character's share of the dialogue. This not only encourages students to get to the meat of the dialogue quickly, but it also lends itself to lessons on proper punctuation and dialogue tags.

One teacher asks students to illustrate and write about the elements of a mystery. Using a combination of clip art, original drawings and photos, student pairs create scenes for mysteries. One picture illustrates "Crime scene," for instance. When the picture is complete, the students collaboratively write the details of the scene, which could be turned into the setting of the story. Students developed pages for "Evidence," and "Solution." In their writing, they use mystery vocabulary words such as perpetrator, suspect, red herring, and investigation. The finished set of pictures forms a mystery plot. In this way, the teacher knows that students understand the elements of a mystery without asking them to write the narrative, which is, for many students, the most difficult story type to write well.

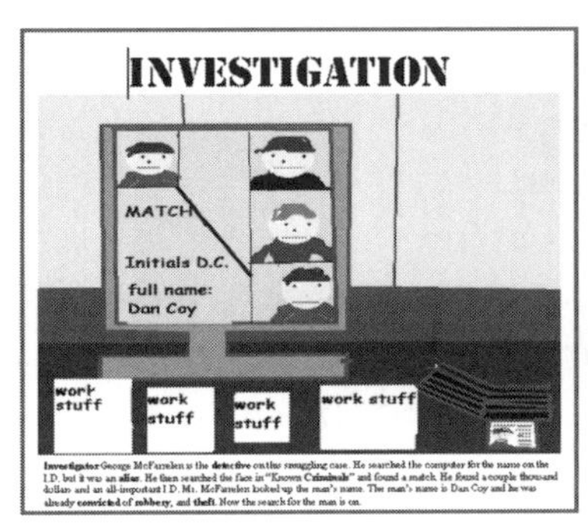

FIGURE 7.6 Fifth-graders Conor and Dylan collaborated on a mystery story. They created their scenes in a drawing program then inserted the pictures into a word-processing program. In text boxes, they explained the progress of the mystery to its conclusion. Their pictures and explanations demonstrated that they understood the elements and vocabulary of mysteries.

Group Projects (4–5)

Students can create books, essays, and long word-processed documents when they work in teams. Intermediate-level students collaborate to research and write chapters on aspects of weather extremes, such as earthquakes and volcano eruptions. They assemble the chapters into a book for younger students whose curriculum covers weather. Writing for a real audience motivates students to produce better work.

Famous Patriots-
Arrest on sight.

George Washington - *A planter from Virginia. He once fought alongside British troops in the French and Indian War. He is Commander of the Continental Army.*

Patrick Henry - *A Virginian. Also known as "Son of Thunder" he started making former Tories into Patriots through one of his lines: "Give me liberty or give me death!"*

Paul Revere - *A silversmith. A leader of Sons of Liberty, as a messenger for the Patriots. He made his famous midnight ride April 18, 1775. We caught him once, but he escaped.*

John Adams, Benjamin Franklin, and Thomas Jefferson - *The most well-known fathers of the Declaration of Independence.*

Deborah Sampson - *Dressed in men's clothes and joined the Continental Army and fought in the war.*

TOP SECRET

Patriot Identification Manual.
Loyalist Eyes Only
September 1779
By Krista and Kelly

Patriots are known as, "Rebels, Liberty boys, Sons (or Daughters) of Liberty, Colonials, and Wings."

Bibliography: Moore, Kay ... If You Lived at the Time of The American Revolution. New York Scholastic Inc., 1997.

FIGURE 7.7 In a fifth-grade classroom, pairs of students collaborated on manuals for the soldiers during the Revolutionary War. Krista and Kelly wrote from the perspective of Loyalist leaders about the Patriot fighters.

In some classes, students work in fours to research and write about a curricular topic, such as the Native American tribes from various regions of the country. Each student studies one aspect of life, such as food, traditions, shelter, or clothing, and writes a fact-filled essay. The teams combine their essays to make a large, comprehensive document. Because the individual pieces have different tones and styles, the team then revises the essay to unify the sections.

In a study of the American Revolution, students divide into colonial and British camps. They create documents that may have circulated during the war, such as enemy identification manuals and reports of spying.

Word processing encompasses far more than just a typed report. When teachers and students use word processing creatively to synthesize classroom study, the finished products can demonstrate high levels of thinking and problem solving.

Composing at the Keyboard

Ideally, most students will write a story or report longhand before keying it into a word-processing program. At Lenski, students often write each sentence on a separate strip of paper so that they can reorganize their ideas before they type them. The sentence strips can be taped or glued in place so that they won't dislodge before the student has finished typing.

When students demonstrate that they can organize their thoughts without needing to rearrange the sentence strips, then they may be ready to try composing at the keyboard. Even then, they should use outlines prepared in advance to keep them organized. In my experience, fourth graders may be ready to compose at the computer with only outlines, but any earlier may be too soon. In fact, for many students, fourth grade will be too early.

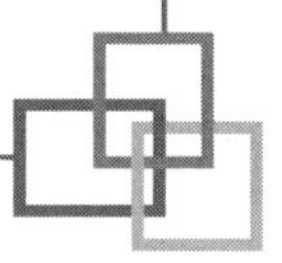

LESSON PLAN

Grade 2, Fossils and Dinosaurs

TEACHERS(S):	COLLABORATIVE PARTNER(S):
Second Grade	Technology Teacher and Media Specialist
CURRICULAR AREA(S):	**CONTENT TARGET(S):**
Science	Identify decomposition and fossilization; predict based on scientific inquiry, recognize that dinosaur fossils are evidence of past life
Language Arts	Taking notes, writing a story, listing facts; reading for varied purposes

STANDARDS ADDRESSED:

National Science Content Standards K–4:

C. Understanding life cycles of organisms and interactions of organisms and environments

National Language Arts Standards:

1. Reading for varied purposes
5. Communicating to audiences
8. Using the research process to gain information

ISTE National Technology Standards:

2. Using productivity tools to enhance learning, promote creativity, and produce creative works
4. Using technology research tools

FINAL PRODUCT:

- Students will complete a WebQuest on dinosaurs that incorporates writing.
- Students will create dinosaur birth announcements about specific dinosaurs they have researched.

Necessary Skills (Content, Technology):

Content:

- Know how fossils are formed, that fossils are a record of history; that our knowledge of dinosaurs comes from fossils
- Know note-taking strategies and conventions of expository text

Technology:

- Using a drawing program, navigating an Internet site, typing in a template; saving files, inserting and manipulating graphics, changing decorative text, and printing two-sided files

TIMELINE:

DATE:	PERSON RESPONSIBLE:	ACTIVITY:
WEEK 1	Classroom Teacher	Introduce fossils through two Web sites projected for whole class discussion: Burying Bodies (www.bbc.co.uk/sn/prehistoric_life/dinosaurs/burying_bodies/) and Making Fossils (www.bbc.co.uk/sn/prehistoric_life/dinosaurs/making_fossils/). With a projector, introduce the Using the Web to Research Dinosaurs Web site (www.childrensmuseum.org/dinosphere/games/reader/reader_activity_step1.htm), which is an activity in the Dinosphere at The Children's Museum of Indianapolis. Teachers will need to make copies of the worksheets or, better yet, show students how to toggle between the activity and a computer copy of the worksheets. Assign students to work in pairs or triplets to complete the WebQuest.
	Media Specialist and Classroom Teacher	In the library and classroom, students use library books about dinosaurs, the Dino Dictionary (www.dinodictionary.com) and Beyond T. rex (www.ology.amnh.org/paleontology/cladogram/index.html) to learn and take notes about dinosaurs of their choice.
	Technology Teacher	In lab setting, introduce the dinosaur birth announcement template and help students save a copy to their files.
	Technology and Classroom Teachers	Assist students as they draw pictures of their dinosaurs. If students complete their pictures before class ends, permit them to insert the pictures into the birth announcement template and begin typing the text.

Week 2	Classroom Teacher	Continue providing time and materials so that students can read and write about dinosaurs. Introduce Stories From the Fossil Record (www.ucmp.berkeley.edu/education/explorations/tours/stories/middle/intro.html) for computer rotation time. Students can explore one or more stories in pairs and note important information to include in their writing journals.
	Both Teachers	In the lab, students complete the fronts and backs of the birth announcement. Teachers help the students group the elements to copy and paste them so that the students have a total of eight frames. These can then be printed on a duplex printer. If the school does not have a duplex printer, then the student needs only four frames and can print once, turn the cards over and print again on the back side of the paper.
Week 3	Classroom Teacher	If additional time is needed to complete projects or to explore the Web sites, the classroom teacher will provide time during reading or science.

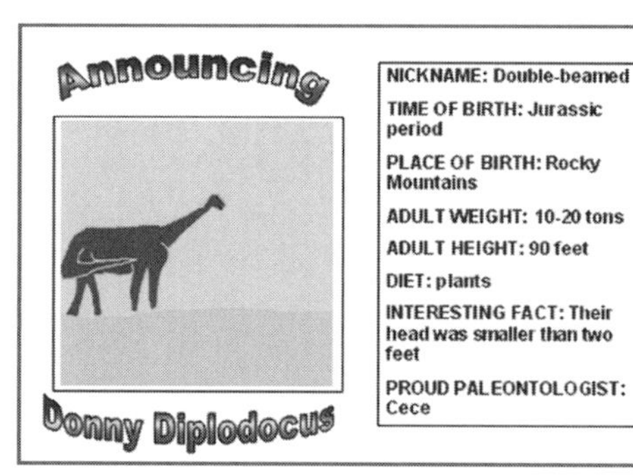

FIGURE 7.8 For this dinosaur birth announcement, Cece filled in a template with her own text and picture. She drew the picture of her dinosaur in a drawing program and inserted it. The information on the reverse of the card came from her notes. The template for postcards can be created either in word processing by setting up the page for Avery labels 5845 Note card, Mtg. Creator or in presentation software by turning on the guidelines that divide the page into four sections. When the card is printed on two sides, the student ends up with four cards. Avery makes a perforated postcard paper that is available from discount houses at reasonable prices.

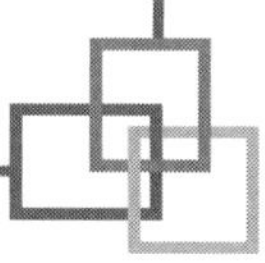

Chapter 8

Word Processing to Improve Writing

THE INCREASE OF STATE TESTING forces teachers to think about how they teach writing. For teachers who did not receive adequate writing instruction themselves, becoming good teachers of writing requires thoughtful attention to what constitutes good writing.

Many of the programs intended to help teachers improve their writing instruction also seem to create bland and formulaic writing. The problem is not the method; the formulas have been in existence for decades, if not centuries. As a college junior in my first writing class, I learned the same organizational patterns that first and second graders use today. However, because of my intellectual maturity and experience, I needed little time to grasp the formula frameworks and advance my writing to a higher level.

Students in Grades K–2 take longer to master the organizational patterns of writing. They need time to practice building writing structures—and at times their voices may seem stifled. In truth, if you look at primary students' writing that has lots of voice, it typically also has lots of problems—in organization, syntax, consistency of detail, or sentence variety. What we typically enjoy about young student writing is the spontaneity that infuses it, not the excellence of the writing. While we want to preserve that spontaneity, we

Step Up to Writing Program

As schools struggle to improve their writing programs, they often turn to experts to provide staff development on what makes good writers.

All Lenski teachers have received training in the use of the Step Up to Writing program (www.stepuptowriting.com). In this program, students use colors to identify the key elements of their paragraphs as an aid to organization. Initially, students write on colored strips of paper as a kinesthetic experience to reinforce the purposes of the colors. This writing on strips begins as early as kindergarten. Students can move the strips to reorganize them as needed. Eventually, the strips can be glued or attached with adhesive spray to a base.

As students gain competency with organizing their writing, they often outline in colors and compose their paragraphs at the keyboard. They can then recheck their work by changing the font colors for each sentence.

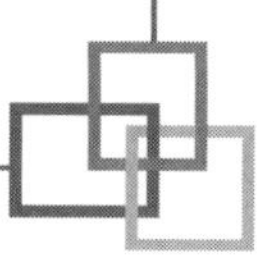

have a responsibility to help students mature so that their writing not only has voice but also communicates well.

At Lenski, where we use the organizational frameworks of a writing program called Step Up to Writing, we accept that formulas are an essential foundation for becoming an excellent writer. Just as the beginning musician practices scales first, the beginning writer works on paragraph structures first. Teachers help novice writers master the basics and then encourage them to explore writing beyond the basics.

Your school may use a different framework for helping students organize and improve their writing. The importance lies not in the specific training program, but the consistency of writing instruction. Within a school, all staff should use the same language and techniques during writing instruction. Teachers also need to model writing techniques before they ask students to practice them.

Word processing can help students dramatically improve their writing.

Planning Before Writing

Many schools use computer software, particularly purchased programs specifically designed for pre-writing, to help students organize their thoughts. (See Curriculum Mapping Software sidebar in the Introduction.) They speak highly of the software, and it clearly has found a place in many schools. Schools that want to use computers for graphic organizers and cannot afford specialty software could consider using the Autoshape tools in spreadsheets and presentation programs (see chapters 10 and 11).

Coloring Expository Text

Because Lenski staff members teach writing through the framework of Step Up to Writing, our students use colors to identify the specific parts of their paragraphs: blue for a grabber opening; green for the topic and concluding sentences; yellow (gold) for reasons, examples and explanations; and red for details. Other writing programs use different colors, but they all use the same parts of the paragraph. Again, the important issue is consistency within a school, not the specific color combination. Students use different colors to identify the different purposes of sentences: opening, topic sentence, supporting sentences, and details.

Our students write their sentences on colored paper strips and organize them by either gluing them to a blank sheet of paper or sticking them to a file folder treated with adhesive spray. The colored strips help students write one sentence at a time, pay attention to each sentence's purpose, and reorganize easily, if necessary.

Color-coding, whether with strips or word-processed text, allows students (and teachers) to quickly assess whether the paragraph is organized and where a student can make improvements. Paragraphs should have at least two supporting (in our case, yellow) sentences. If they don't, students should either broaden

RESOURCES

Curriculum Mapping Resources

While the Lenski staff and I used spreadsheet software to create our curriculum maps, schools can use mapping software to design their own. Options include:

Inspiration (www.inspiration.com). A popular software package for schools, teachers can use the templates or create their own. Students can add a variety of objects to a page. The software can auto-arrange the bubbles and can create outlines from the graphic layout. Inspiration costs $69 for one package and almost $900 for twenty.

CMap (http://cmap.ihmc.us/Index.html). A free download, CMap Tools is a concept-mapping tool created for university-level research and released for others to use. CMap uses concepts, linking words, and propositions to visually diagram relationships among concepts. The Web site has a knowledge base for support and several public servers that store concept maps for educational institutions.

Belvedere (http://belvedere.sourceforge.net/). Designed originally to help secondary students develop critical inquiry thinking skills, Belvedere is now available freely as open-source software. People around the globe contribute updates and improvements to the software periodically. Belvedere has simple tools and a strong online support community. Users can diagram concept or evidence models, and information can be presented as maps or graphs.

their topics or develop additional support. Each yellow (supporting) sentence needs one or more red detail sentences. If the reds are missing, writers should consider whether they need to do more research, add a personal experience, or even combine two yellows into one broader statement.

Until fourth grade, students write on sentence strips, organize their writing, and then type from the strips. In fourth and fifth grades, our students typically write paragraphs as a whole without color strips, but after they word-process the writing, they often color-code the sentences for evaluation. A color-coded document, whether evaluated onscreen or printed, simplifies assessing and revising a student's organizational plan.

Students ask peers to read their color-coded text to evaluate whether the paragraphs are organized and balanced with sufficient detail. Only after one to three peers have read the text is it ready for a teacher's eyes.

Text to Table Conversion

Our students don't stop after color-coding their text. In order to do more sophisticated text evaluation, students convert their paragraphs to one-column tables where each sentence has its own cell. The conversion offers multiple new ways to assess and revise text.

While the process of converting from text to table takes manipulation that may challenge students at first, its benefits outweigh the difficulties. When students complete the conversion, every sentence of the text has its own line.

When students look at their text one line at a time in a table, they see patterns that elude them otherwise. The following list of mini-lessons should be modeled

If I could wish upon a star my only wish would be to go to New York. First, I would get to go in to the city and eat the famous New York hot dogs. In addition, I would like to see the Statue of Liberty with my family. The most important, would be to get to see my old blue house and my other friends. **I miss not seeing them. As you can see, I would wish to go to New York.**

If I could wish upon a star, my only wish would be to go to New York
First, New York has wonderful hot dogs and I want to eat one
I've bought hot dogs in the grocery store, and I think a real New York style dog must taste even better.
The juicy hot dogs are great with mustard and ketchup.
Their aroma must tempt the people coming out of the subway
I imagine shoving through the crowd to find a hot dog stand
In addition, I want to see the Statue of Liberty with my family
Picnicking in the shadow of the Statue of Liberty could be a great experience

FIGURE 8.1 Emma, a third grader, wrote the paragraph at the top in response to a writing prompt. She and her classmates thought the paragraph was well written when they saw it in this format. Then Emma gave permission for the class to work collectively on a revision. They focused on two problem areas: adding detail and varying sentence beginnings. In half an hour, they came up with the revised paragraph at the bottom based on Emma's answers to their questions.

Text to Table Conversion Process in Microsoft Word

1. Highlight the text of the paragraph.
2. Go to **Table** > **Convert Text to Table**.
3. For **Separate text at:** choose **Other** and type a **period** in the box.
4. For **Number of Columns**, type **1**.
5. Click **OK**.

The table will have a sentence in each row.

Adaptation: Simplify the process for younger or less computer-savvy students in the following way:

1. Use the **Edit** > **Replace** tool to change all exclamation marks and question marks to periods.
2. Select all the text.
3. Use the **Edit** > **Replace** tool to change all periods to periods followed by three Returns. The return is typed as ^p.
4. The sentences will be spread out so that students can work on one sentence at a time.
5. When improvements have been made, use the **Edit** > **Replace** tool to replace all periods and three Returns (^p) with periods and a space.
6. Proofread to determine whether any periods should be changed back to exclamation marks or question marks.

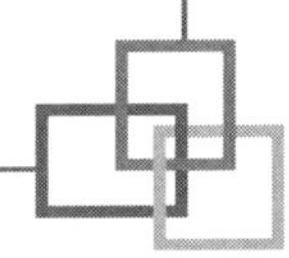

one at a time, practiced, and gradually added to expectations. In younger grades, teachers may use writing samples in table form for whole group instruction on some of the simpler techniques. Beginning in Grade 3, teachers can use students' writing to demonstrate these techniques. Remember to focus on one skill at a time, model it multiple times, and give lots of practice before expecting students to incorporate the skill. These mini-lessons are not in any particular order; teachers start with a skill their students can manage.

- Text organization: Students read every sentence to determine whether it is in the correct place in the paragraph. Any row can be moved to reorganize the text.
- Expansion of text: Students can insert a row at any point in the table and add sentences. Inserting a row into a table is easier for some students than adding a sentence to a traditional paragraph.

- Subject-Verb: Every sentence has a subject and a verb. All verbs should be the same tense. All subjects and verbs should agree in number.
- Sentence length: Good writing varies the length of sentences.
- Transitions: Once students have learned to organize well, they should drop the transitional words. In my experience, when the transition words are gone, students almost instinctively revise sentences with buried and implied transitions, an abstract skill difficult to teach.
- Sentence beginnings: When many sentences start with the same words, the paragraph suffers.
- Spelling and grammar corrections: Looking at one sentence at a time enables the student to focus on the words.
- Verb choice: Adding sparkle means adding strong, lively verbs, not adjectives and adverbs. Replace overused verbs such as go, love, have, and get with livelier words.
- Vocabulary use: Through the regular use of vocabulary words in writing, the students truly absorb the words into their personal word banks. Using rich vocabulary and particularly lively verbs adds voice.

Reverting From Table to Text

When students have completed their corrections and revisions, they need to convert the table back to text. This procedure may seem complex at first, but students find it easy to learn.

Teachers may want students to print both the original and the revised text so that students can see how much their revisions improved their work.

Improving Narrative Writing

Teachers can use a similar process for narrative writing. If color-coding adds value for your students, create a color code for narrative as well. Some writing teachers recommend using different colors so that students remember the difference between narrative and expository writing. The parts that could be highlighted are

1. Grabber opening and wrap-up
2. Story elements, such as place, time, character names, and central problem, as well as resolution
3. Changes in time, place or problem
4. Action

Reverting from Table to Text in Microsoft Word

Make sure the cursor is blinking in a table cell.

1. Go to **Table** > **Select Table.**
2. Go to **Table** > **Convert Table to Text**.
3. For **Separate text at:** choose **Paragraph Mark**.
4. Click **OK**. The text will have one paragraph mark (¶) after each sentence and two paragraph marks (¶ ¶) after each paragraph.
5. Immediately, while the text is still highlighted, go to **Edit** > **Replace**.
6. Type **^p** in the **Find what:** box.
7. Type a period in the **Replace with:** box.
8. Click **Replace All**. This will put a period and one space after each sentence.
9. With all text still highlighted, go back to **Edit** > **Replace**.
10. Type **two periods** (no space between them) in the **Find what:** box.
11. Type **one period** then **^p** (no space between them) in the **Replace with:** box.
12. Click **Replace All**. This will insert paragraph separations back into the text.

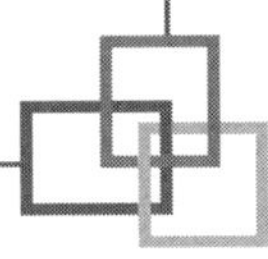

When students convert this to a table, they will not only look at the factors listed above, but at a few other elements that make fiction effective:

- Problem: In fiction, the problem must be within the main character's power to solve.
- Complications: A good story has a central problem that might be solvable except that the main character's choices result in making things worse.
- Dialogue: Fictional dialogue differs from conversation because it must be concise and still sound authentic. To improve their use of dialogue, students can take a play script and convert it to prose with dialogue, including dialogue tags and actions.
- Resolution of the problem: The problem either gets solved by the main character or defeats the main character. That's why problems must be simple.
- Characters: Limit students to no more than three characters in a short story. Using a character Web as illustrated in chapter 10 might help.
- Point of view: Students will have more success with third-person point of view and past tense. Whatever they choose, their story should stay consistent.

Additional Tools and Techniques

Often students complain that they can't think of a topic, or a teacher would like help in designing a unique writing prompt. WritingFix (www.writingfix.com) offers a wealth of writing ideas, particularly the random prompt generators. Prompts are organized by the writing traits, or right- and left-brain thinking. The purpose of the site is to spark creativity and to encourage everyone to write every day.

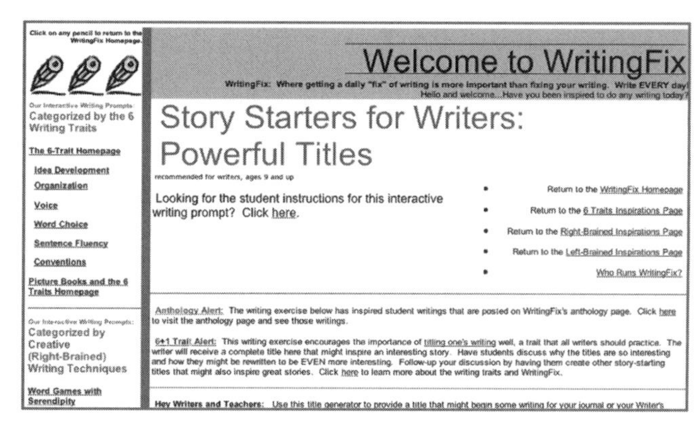

FIGURE 8.2 Although WritingFix is text-heavy for a Web site, the tools and information within the site can inspire even the most reluctant writers. The random prompt generators sometimes create crazy prompts, but eventually, any writer can find a combination that lights a spark.

Lenski teachers continually improve as teachers of writing as they share their ideas and best instructional practices during weekly staff development. In fact, talking about how using tables to improve students' awareness of flaws in their writing led to a recent "aha" moment for me.

For years, I have told students to edit and revise their work. In my mind I am saying edit (correct) and revise (improve) as two separate processes, but students define the phrase as one word: fix. Often students use an editing strategy such as COPS (Capitalization, Overall appearance and readability, Punctuation, and Spelling) and declare their work done, having made no improvement to the writing itself.

Even when students recognize the difference between editing and revision, they resist making revisions. For the struggling writers, the editing process is so arduous that they can't imagine how much work actual improvement to their writing will take. Advanced writers consider their work so superior to what others are writing that they don't see the necessity for improvement.

Now that I consciously recognize why students often don't revise their work, I've begun talking differently. Students edit their work first. They use editing strategies and tools. COPS works as one editing strategy. Another editing strategy is using the spelling checker, although students' success with this tool is highly variable.

As a tool for those who can spell already, the spelling checker helps with troublesome words such as silhouette or words that end in -able or -ible. For students and adults who struggle with spelling even common words, the use of the spelling checker can make a document worse, rather than better.

Students can begin to use the spelling checker in the second grade, but its use should be explicitly taught so that students learn how to evaluate the suggestions. Without instruction on how to use this tool, some students click on Ignore or, even worse, Add to Dictionary, if they don't recognize the alternative words being offered. This removes the annoying misspelling red lines but doesn't correct the words. To give students practical experience, teachers can create documents with intentional examples of easily confused words or mistakes that the computer might miss with the limitations of the spelling checker. Students need to understand that the spell check function only helps when the spelling of the word is close or when the writer chooses carefully from the list of options.

One way to improve the spelling checker function is to download the 1-Click Answers from www.Answers.com. Answers Corporation aggregates dictionary and encyclopedia information from many sources for one-stop shopping for information. One of their free downloads is 1-Click Answers, an interface that enables Windows and Mac clients to hold down the Alt key and left-click on any word in order to bring up the definition. When students aren't certain that they have chosen the right word from spell check, they can Alt-click on their choice and get a definition and pronunciation.

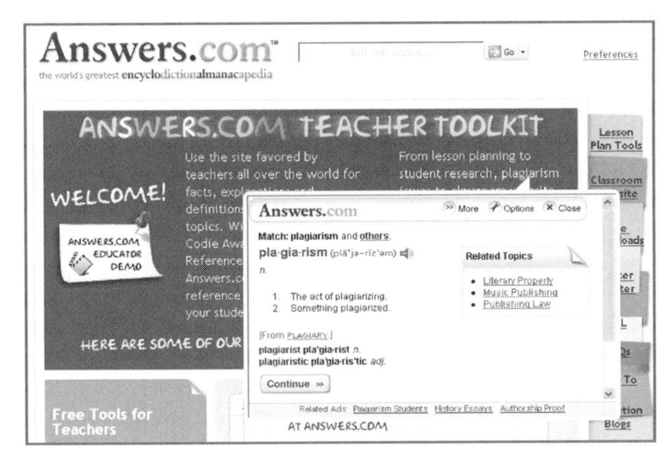

FIGURE 8.3 Once 1-Click Answers has been installed on a computer, bringing up the definition and pronunciation of a word is as easy as holding down the Alt key and left-clicking on the word. Students can check words they've chosen from the spelling checker with the 1-Click Answers tool.

After students have edited their work, they should revise. I tell students when they edit, they are making sure they look good to others, like dressing up for school pictures. When they revise, they improve their writing for the reader's sake. Good writers add figurative language, clarify confusing passages, and sharpen the word choices to be more precise. Everyone can improve, so no one should declare his/her writing finished until at least three revisions or improvements have been made. Placing a limit on how many revisions a student must make eases the burden. Most students think that three changes won't be hard to do and won't make much difference. Yet, once they see how easy it is to improve and how much of a difference each improvement makes, students often make additional changes to their work. The number of minimum improvements is, of course, completely up to the teacher and may differ from student to student.

In my experience, students have less success using the grammar tool than spell check. If teachers wish to ask upper elementary students to check for grammar, then it would be wise first to customize the grammar checker to look for specific items. In my experience, the more complex the text, the more likely the grammar checker will be wrong. However, if students tend to overlook fragments or subject-verb agreement, customizing the grammar checker to identify those will help make students aware of problems. The use of the grammar checker should also be taught explicitly to students so they understand the messages and don't click Change indiscriminately.

The built-in thesaurus can help students vary their word choice in writing. For simple, overused words, the thesaurus can often suggest alternatives that will perk up the students' writing. Explicit instruction on effective use of the thesaurus will help students see that many words have more than one meaning, so not all suggestions will be appropriate. Thesaurus use should complement and support a strong vocabulary program in the classroom.

Teaching the writing process to students intimidates many teachers who don't consider themselves strong writers. Using technology to help students evaluate and improve their own writing has given Lenski teachers more confidence as they work with students on the writing process.

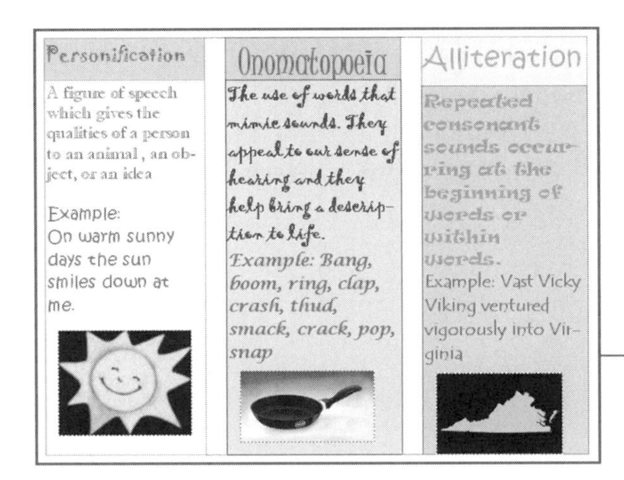

Chapter 9

Desktop Publishing

AS THIS BOOK ILLUSTRATES, students can publish books, folders, and cards with productivity software, however, a desktop publishing program often provides options that the productivity software lacks.

Some office productivity software comes with a desktop publishing component. In that case, the similarity between word processing and desktop publishing will probably be negligible, so students can use the publishing option frequently.

However, if desktop publishing is not part of the productivity suite, then consider carefully whether students will use the software often enough to warrant the additional expense, especially since the most common tasks done in a publishing software can be replicated in productivity software. An independent desktop publishing program will probably look significantly different from the basic software students typically use. That means students must have enough time to learn the new tools and procedures for the publishing software. In fact, teachers often choose to limit students' independence in desktop publishing in order to save time. Instead of creating each publishing project from scratch, it may be easiest to create a template with default text boxes and pictures. Students replace the words and, if there is time, pictures with their own choices, but they don't add any elements to the template. Even with that level of support, a simple greeting card can easily take an hour.

If students start with templates in the primary grades, then in the intermediate grades, teachers may give them more independence. They may add elements (digital pictures, extra text boxes, etc.) or even build projects from scratch. Their projects generally take at least two hours, and complex products such as books and newsletters may take much longer.

Teachers often like desktop publishing projects because the products lend themselves to authentic purposes. Whether students make cards for their parents or write books for younger students, they love knowing that someone besides the teacher will see and appreciate their work. That often motivates students to do their best work.

Quarter-fold Cards (1–5)

Although students can make quarter-fold cards in standard word-processing and presentation programs, desktop publishing makes the process easier and less frustrating because each quarter page is separated in order on the screen. Students can create greeting cards for many reasons, including holidays, celebrations, or thank-you notes. Younger students do best when they have a template.

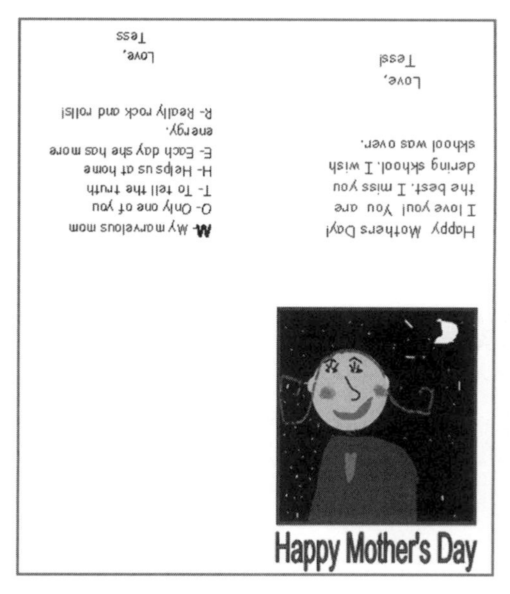

FIGURE 9.1 First-grader Tess used an original drawing of her mother for the front of a Mother's Day card. The inside had two styles of writing: a note and an acrostic. Although this could be done in presentation software by turning the text boxes upside down, using a teacher-created template in a desktop publishing program made it easier for Tess to focus on what she wanted to say.

Intermediate students can learn how to add or alter elements on a template at first. This gives them the background knowledge they need to create a card from a blank page on subsequent projects.

Students can add personal touches to cards as well. For instance, they can first draw illustrations for their cards in a painting program. When students import their illustrations into quarter-fold cards, the picture shrinks by as much as 75%. The resultant pictures have finer details than students could create if they tried to draw pictures that small. One teacher has used cards illustrated with students' drawings for thank-you notes to parents. Another has created card sets to auction off as a fund-raiser.

Books (2–5)

Desktop publishing programs offer flexibility for creating books. Students can make quarter-fold page books and have the pages print on a duplex printer in the right order for folding and stapling. Students may also create double-fold or full-page books.

Whether the book is fiction or non-fiction, students must determine how much text goes on each page and plan their illustrations to match the text. Illustrations can be clip art, photographs, or drawings. In some classes, teachers create storyboards to help students plan their pages.

Having a genuine audience will improve students' work. Possibilities include picture books illustrated with digital photography on topics such as opposites, shapes, or colors. These can be shared with kindergarten buddies to reinforce curricular units. Fifth graders create books about the colonial period and present them to second graders when the second-grade unit on colonial life begins. Fourth graders write fiction, which they read to their first-grade buddies.

One second-grade teacher asks her students to create books about the inventions they make. The books give explanations of how their inventions work, descriptions of the students' thought and inventing processes, and biographies of the inventors. Such an ambitious project with primary students requires substantial support and time, but students treasure the finished products. The second-grade students place their books next to their inventions at the Invention Convention.

Promotional Flyers (3–5)

Students (and staff) can create flyers to promote activities or events. For instance, one third-grade class creates flyers for Earth Day and promotes the three R's: Reduce, Reuse, Recycle. Student council members advertise charity drives and school elections. Promotional flyers can also be used by the school staff to announce parent education events.

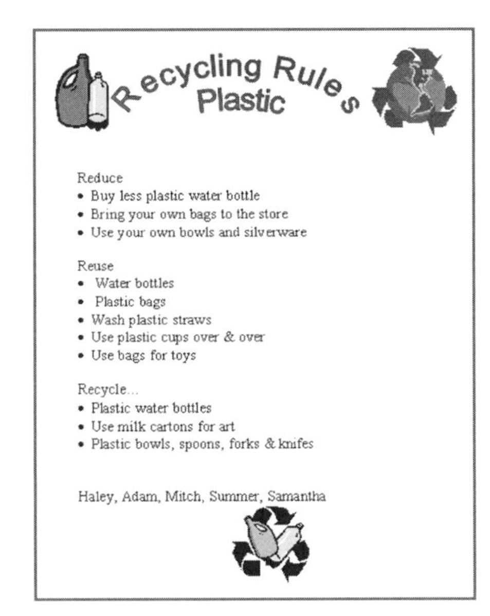

FIGURE 9.2 Third-grade students focused on plastics for their Earth Day flyer. They posted the flyers around the school to remind their peers about the three Rs of recycling.

Brochures (4–5)

Brochures are especially suited for health units. Fifth-grade students have created brochures about nutrition, dental care, smoking, alcohol abuse, and organ or tissue donation. They research these topics and struggle to find effective ways to present the research without being dry or wordy. They learn about eye-catching titles and illustrations, precise language, and correct citations of sources. Teachers use library card pockets attached to the wall near the classroom to display the students' work. This way the brochures have an additional purpose of reaching students with health messages.

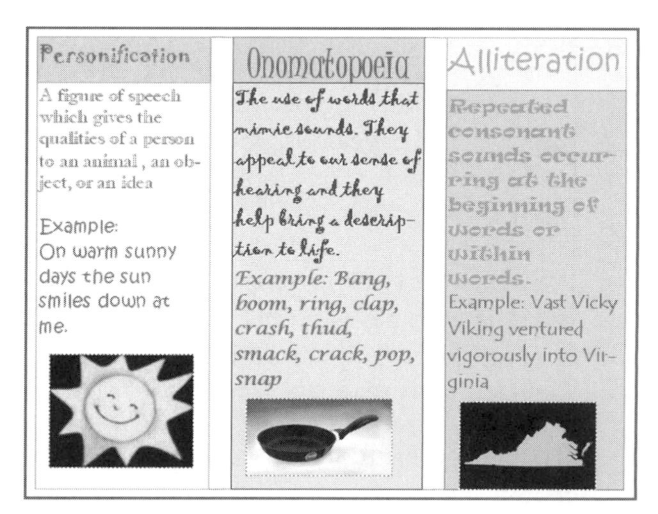

FIGURE 9.3 Natalie's brochure about figurative language has large text, colorful backgrounds, and plain pictures to present difficult vocabulary simply.

Because brochures are informational or marketing tools, students can create brochures for practically any curricular unit. Imagine advertising a state or tourist area, advocating conservation, explaining the types of rocks, teaching others how to prevent accidents, advertising for a wagon train headed for the Northwest Territory, or giving an overview of the Apollo space program.

Newspapers (4–5)

When fourth-grade students study state history, one favorite activity is creating a newspaper with the news of the times. Especially effective is having groups of students produce newspapers from different perspectives (miners, businessmen, settlers, ranchers, etc.). What is headline news to one group may garner a scathing editorial from another. Newspapers require significantly more time than many teachers can devote, but they are excellent opportunities for assessing students' synthesis skills.

Students love to create projects that look complex but are within their ability. Desktop publishing software takes the complexity out of books, brochures, and cards. Each of these projects can be managed in other applications, but desktop publishing makes the projects easier.

LESSON PLAN

Grade 4, Native Americans and Regions of the U.S.

Teachers(s):	Collaborative Partner(s):
Fourth Grade	Technology Teacher
Curricular Area(s):	**Content Target(s):**
Social Studies	Examine influences of cultures on U.S. regions; understand the past and its impact on the world today; collect information from electronic resources
Language Arts	Understand legends; make use of information from a variety of sources; expand vocabulary

Standards Addressed:

National Social Studies Standards:

I. Understanding how culture and experience influence perspectives of place

National Language Arts Standards:

1. Reading for varied purposes
5. Communicating to audiences
8. Using the research process to gain information
9. Multicultural understanding.

ISTE National Technology Standards:

1. Practicing responsible use of information
2. Using productivity tools to produce creative work
4. Using technology to locate and evaluate information

Final Product:

- In teams of four or five, students will create a multimedia presentation that highlights the geographic features of the region that influenced how a Native American tribe lived. In their research, students will consider clothing, shelter, food, tasks, art, and cultural beliefs and practices.
- Students will write a legend based on their research about the culture and practices of a Native American tribe that lived in a specific region of the U.S.

Necessary Skills (Content, Technology, Information Literacy):

Content:

- Know the customs, beliefs, and lifestyles of a Native American tribe from a specific region of the U.S.
- Know the characteristics of a legend
- Know the meanings of geography terms, vocabulary words, and key Native American terms, such as tipi and maize, when appropriate

Technology:

- Know how to locate, evaluate, and synthesize information from multiple electronic sources
- Know the tools and processes of multimedia presentations
- Know the tools and processes of a desktop publishing application
- Know the processes of converting text to table and reverting back to text
- Know word-processing skills and keyboarding techniques

TIMELINE:

DATES	PERSON RESPONSIBLE:	ACTIVITY:
WEEK 1	Classroom Teacher	Divide students into teams of four or five and assign each team a region of the U.S. for research. The teams will use text and electronic databases to gather information about a specific Native American tribe located in the region.
	Media Specialist	Review visual literacy with primary source photographs from the Library of Congress collection of Edward S. Curtis's The North American Indians: Photographic Images (http://memory.loc.gov/ammem/award98/ienhtml/tribes.html). Select a few photographs from the site to let students make comparisons between their lives and the lives of the people in the pictures. Students can infer from the pictures where the Native Americans may have lived, what the climate was like, why the housing wass built in a particular way, etc. This will prepare them for making the connections between the geographic features of the region and the lives of the people. Review the resources for research on Native American tribes. Resources should include print materials, library (school or public) subscription-based research databases, the Library of Congress, and Answers.com. An additional informational site is Native American Sites (www.nativeculturelinks.com/indians.html), which lists links to the Web sites of many Native American tribes.
	Classroom Teacher and Media Specialist	Provide a graphic organizer or review note-taking strategies. Brainstorm questions that students will want to answer in their research. Allot time for teams to divide responsibilities and conduct research.

WEEK 2	Classroom and Technology Teachers	Show an abridged teacher sample of a multimedia presentation. Review any skills that students may lack. Guide teams though creating the master slide in a presentation software application. Enroll students in an online collaborative working space such as Nicenet or Multiply (chapter 12).
	Classroom Teacher	Allot time for collaborative work. Students should have their research completed by midweek and be working on their presentations.
WEEK 3	Classroom Teacher	Introduce the characteristics of legends. Use printed and online resources to provide sample legends that students can analyze and imitate. Online sources include Oban's Myths, Legends and Fables (www.planetozkids.com/oban/legends.htm) or Myths and Legends of the Sioux (http://etext.lib.virginia.edu/toc/modeng/public/McIMyth.html). Instruct teams to work collaboratively to outline the plot of a legend that would fit what they know of their Native American tribe. The story must involve an animal indigenous to the region of the U.S. Although students plot their stories as a team, they write individually. Students may work on their legends while teammates complete their contributions to the multimedia presentation. Allot time for working on projects. Students compose their legends in a word-processing program so that they can convert the text to table format for editing and revision.
WEEK 4	Classroom and Technology Teachers	Review the tools and processes for publishing in a desktop publishing program. Students copy and paste their legends into the publishing program, add pictures, titles, and bibliographies, and print.
	Classroom Teacher	Students continue their work on both projects in class. When they have finished their work, the teams present their multimedia show to the class.

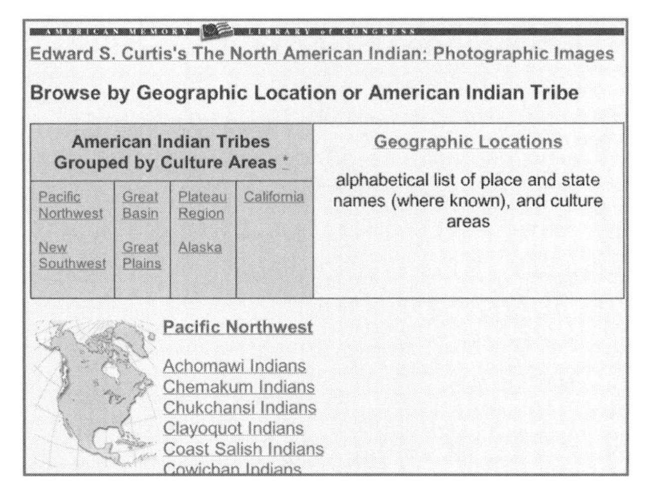

FIGURE 9.4 Edward S. Curtis's The North American Indians: Photographic Images contains photographs and commentary from 1907 to 1930. While the commentary reflects the prejudices of the time, the photographs themselves give viewers insights to cultural traditions of Native American tribes. Selecting a tribe will bring up pictures from that tribe, which will be helpful for students in their multimedia presentations. Switch to gallery view in order to see thumbnail sketches of the photographs.

FIGURE 9.5 Oban's Myths, Legends and Fables generates high interest in Oban the Knowledge Keeper's legends through embellishments and dialogue. His audience for the tales is storytellers, but students will enjoy them as examples of how to add life and color to a legend.

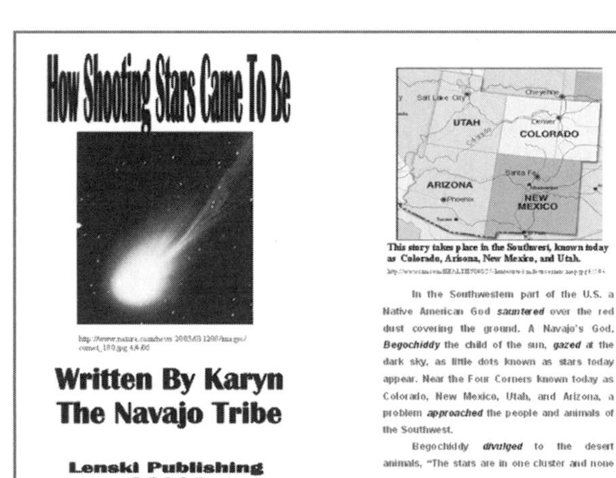

FIGURE 9.6 Karyn's legend about shooting stars includes facts from her research (purple type), vocabulary words (black type), citations for pictures (gray) and color-coding for organization (other type). She has used the animals that live in the region as characters. Students are always surprised that even though they wrote a common plot, which simplifies the storywriting for struggling writers, their stories are very different from one another.

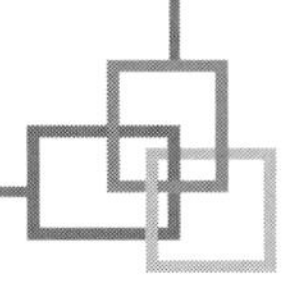

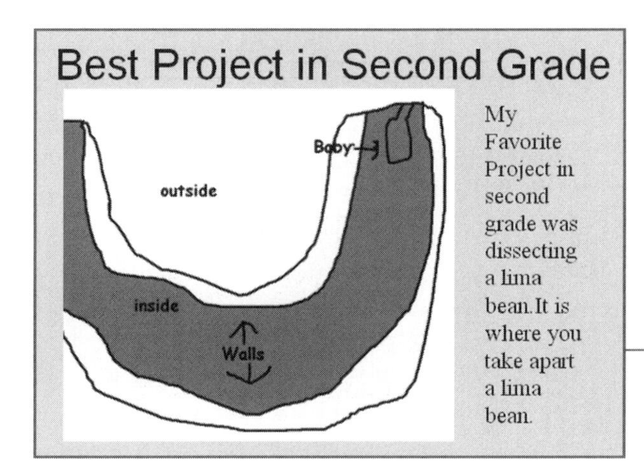

Chapter 10

Presentation Software

MANY TEACHERS HAVE DISCOVERED that presentation software (e.g. PowerPoint) has benefits in the classroom. The intuitive nature and versatility of the software application makes it a natural for a wide variety of projects, not just slide shows. In fact, presentation software may be more versatile than any other office productivity suite application.

Teacher Use

In the classroom teachers can use presentation software as an instructional tool to introduce new material, generate questions, and encourage higher-level thinking.

A slide show developed for instruction often doesn't resemble the slide shows generated by businesses or students. Instead of serving as a background for a lecture or presentation, instructional slide shows invite participation from students.

When students lack background knowledge for a new curricular unit, instructional slide shows can outline the key ideas or use visuals to stimulate questions and discussion among students. Teachers use slide shows for the introduction of vocabulary, review of the previous day's concepts, or demonstration of a lab technique. Want to review before a test? Try a slide show based on a popular television show such as *Jeopardy!*.

Presentations with only visuals (no text) force students to practice inferential skills as they wrestle to understand how what they see relates to what they are learning. Teachers can use maps, charts, labeled drawings, photographs, or video clips to ignite curiosity and to reach students with different learning styles. And because teachers often teach the same units annually, a well-designed slide show can be used year after year and yet be individualized to the personality and needs of a class by simply customizing the commentary and discussion.

Lenski's media specialist has created a 60-slide presentation on volcanoes, a topic that fourth graders study every year. For classes with little background knowledge, the pictures serve as catalysts for questions and discovery. Sometimes the librarian may select only a portion of the show in order to target a particular learning goal. Students with plenty of background knowledge move through the show quickly, and the librarian highlights only the new or challenging areas.

A fifth-grade teacher uses a slide show of photographs and maps to give students background knowledge for a novel that is set in Venice. He then uses GoogleEarth to demonstrate the topography of the city. The students become engaged with the text quickly because they have a context on which to anchor the book's scenes.

In order to use slide shows as an instructional tool, teachers need access to LCD projectors. In the years before Lenski could equip every classroom with LCD projectors, we kept several projectors and laptops on rolling carts, and teachers reserved them for classroom use. While not perfect, it did make the use of technology for instruction possible. Another option is a connection between the computer and a television. This doesn't give as clear a picture as a projector, but in many schools, the price makes it feasible as a temporary solution.

Student Use Overview

The appropriate use for presentation software in a school is limited only by a teacher's creativity. Many presentation software packages are simple to learn and use, and presenting materials visually makes the information easier for many learners to remember.

Students can create presentations to demonstrate their understanding of curricular learning goals or to practice public speaking. For some projects, students make several slides; for others, they each contribute one slide for a comprehensive class presentation. Traditionally, student presentations have a high ratio of pictures to words. The pictures keep the audience engaged and the use of limited bullets compels the speakers to talk, rather than read, to audiences. Students use original art, clip art,

Effective Instructional Slideshows

USE LARGE, CLEAR, AND MEANINGFUL VISUALS. Whether you use photographs, video clips, maps, or diagrams, make them as large as possible so that all students can see them clearly. Generally, that means one visual per page.

Be selective about the visuals you use as well. Choose items that are content-rich and will stimulate discussion, which generally eliminates clip art. Students use clip art as a decorative touch or a memory jogger on their shows, but they are not generally creating instructional tools. Eliminate any clutter that doesn't advance your curricular goals.

The Internet provides rich resources for stimulating visuals, particularly the Library of Congress digital library (www.loc.gov). Subscription-based video streaming services can also be mined for thought-provoking video clips.

Since video clips often have both sound and visuals, if you use video clips to enhance your teaching, consider showing the clips more than once to allow students to absorb all the information. I generally pose a question to set a purpose for watching the video before I play a clip. For a clip about insects in a pond, such as *Insect Life in a Desert Pond* (www.pbs.org/americanfieldguide/index.html) from the American Field Guide Web site, I ask students to pay attention to the levels, or strata, of pond life. After the first viewing, we discuss not only the strata but also other information we noticed. Then we watch the video again so that students can catch what they missed in the earlier viewing. In fact, with information-rich videos, a third or fourth viewing may be appropriate. Just as teachers urge students to read non-fiction texts more than once in order to grasp the nuances, we should approach visual non-fiction the same way. That teaches visual literacy skills as well as content.

LIMIT TEXT. Provide enough text to create a context for the visuals, but don't give all the information through text. The goal is to have students discuss what they learn from the visuals. A teacher who was setting background knowledge for fourth graders about to research Colorado history used photographs from the Library of Congress to generate discussion about the lives of settlers. In addition to the photographs of miners and railroad-building crews, the teacher added the information she had about the years, locations, and purposes of the photos. Students drew conclusions about the lifestyles, social standing, and relationships of the people in the pictures.

Labeling the items in a slide, particularly when the picture is for the purposes of establishing background knowledge, will give students the correct terminology and additional clues about the visual. You can use an AutoShapes with no fill to circle or outline a particular item, and use a connector arrow to attach the AutoShape to a label.

Audio clips are an alternative to text. Photos of people landing on Ellis Island coupled with audio clips of immigrant stories capture the essence of the immigration experience for third graders. The Library of Congress has a wealth of audio and visual resources that can be paired to make history come alive. Podcasts can also enrich slide shows.

INCLUDE UNKNOWNS. Rather than use a slide show as a background for a lecture, design the slide show to introduce unknowns to students. Let them puzzle out how composite and shield volcanoes differ, what characteristics are common among insects,

Continued

or the challenges faced by the Pilgrims. You'll know your slide show is effective if students become so engrossed in understanding the content that they lose track of time.

SKIP THE GLITZ. The "wow" factor of animations and effects lasts for only seconds and then becomes a distraction to students who are more focused on how to replicate the glitz than the content knowledge you are introducing. Remember, the goal is content learning.

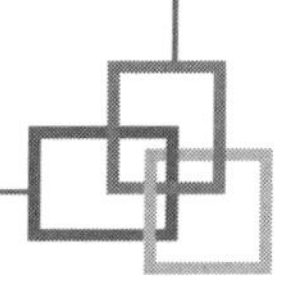

pictures from Internet sites, video clips, or scanned photos. Beginning in late second grade, our students also learn to include the proper citations for the materials they borrow from other sources.

Improving the artistry of presentations requires deliberate instruction. With students in the lower grades, we work on color schemes, layout, and formatting details such as bullets and text styles. Instead of permitting students to select from the pre-designed backgrounds, we ask them to create master slides with pleasing backgrounds and text features.

We reserve animations, slide transitions, and sounds for fourth- and fifth-grade students. Such special effects, when used well, can enhance presentations, but students often can't resist adding so many special effects that the glitz overpowers the message. For instance, I sat through a student presentation where every title came in letter-by-letter accompanied by typing sounds. The bullets and text all came in word-by-word with whoosh sounds. The five-slide show felt interminable, even more so to the student who had to wait for each effect to end before he could speak. While that was the worst show—and his experience prompted several students to make quick changes to the effects on their own shows—I have sat through many other shows where the placement and use of animations and sounds have detracted from rather than complemented the presentations.

On the other hand, a fourth-grade class, given permission to use a limited number of animations in any way they felt would enhance their shows, did an excellent job. One pair of students punctuated their newscast on an active volcano with the rumbling and explosion of an eruption and clip art characters racing for safety.

Not all slide shows need to be presented orally. Teachers can import all of a class's slides into one large presentation. Playing these class shows in an infinite loop in the hall outside the classroom during parent-teacher conferences allows parents to enjoy student work while they wait their turn. It also gives them a sense of the range of abilities and skills within a single classroom.

Replication of Documents and Publishing—Without the Frustration

Practically any project that can be done in word processing or desktop publishing can also be accomplished in presentation software. For instance, bookmarks or brochures done in word-processing programs may frustrate students because clip art jumps around unless students know how to change the formatting. In presentation software, the text boxes and artwork can be manipulated easily and stay wherever the designers place them. Once printed, no one can tell what application has been used.

Presentation software may also be a tool for assessing students, reviewing major learning concepts, and practicing new skills. The following ideas illustrate successful ways students and teachers have used presentation software effectively.

Portfolios (K–5)

Students generate slides throughout the year to illustrate major curricular units. In a drawing program, they illustrate what they have learned and import the illustrations into slides to collect into an ongoing slide show. Alternatively, students can insert photographs of an activity during the unit. The students then add text to explain the illustrations. At the end of the year, the entire slide show can be burned for each child or e-mailed to parents, especially if the school lacks the funds to permit printing the show in color.

FIGURE 10.1 In a slide show about the Best of Second Grade, Ally used a photo of her country research display on the night of the County Af-Fair celebration as an example of a major curricular unit.

Assessing Curricular Skills (K–5)

A teacher can use a four- or five-slide template as an assessment tool. When used in a lab setting, such assessments allow the teachers to circulate among students and assist those who are struggling. When used as a classroom activity, these slide shows can be printed six slides per page to give teachers quick formative assessments.

Kindergarten teachers assess students' mastery of coin recognition with a slide show on sorting coins. The opening slide has four sections surrounding a center diamond. Clip art pictures of coins, both heads and tails, fill the center diamond. Each section on the periphery is designated for a specific coin. Students click on each coin and drag it to the appropriate section.

Each of the first three slides is a duplicate with a different number of coins in the center diamond. That way, students who race through the first slide can continue to be challenged while the teachers work with struggling students. The final slides, designed for the most advanced students, require the students to combine coins to make specific sums less than 15 cents.

In first grade, students sort pictures into equal groups as part of an assessment on fractions. The assessment has seven slides, each with a different number of objects to be divided into equal groups representing common fractions.

A fifth-grade teacher uses a five-slide show with the name of an angle on each slide (acute, obtuse, right, straight, and reflex). On one side of the slide, under the word "Yes," the students draw two examples of that kind of angle. On the other side, under "No," the students draw examples that do not demonstrate the angle. In a text box at the bottom of each slide, students type definitions of the angles. This simple assignment allows the teacher to coach those who are uncertain and to assess all students on the targeted skills. The students enjoy the activity without thinking of it as a test. Other teachers have students draw shapes and define them, illustrate science processes, and interpret graphs presented on the slides.

Bookmarks, Style 1 (1–5)

In presentation software, teachers and students have access to the same Page Setup tools as in word processing. To make a pair of bookmarks, turn the page orientation to portrait rather than the default landscape. Make a template where the page is divided into half. Each half is treated as one side of the bookmark. Students use text boxes, original illustrations, decorative lettering, and photographs to make a front and back for the bookmark. They can advertise a favorite book, author, or activity. When printed two-sided and cut apart, the page becomes two bookmarks. Students can keep one and the other can go into either the classroom or school library.

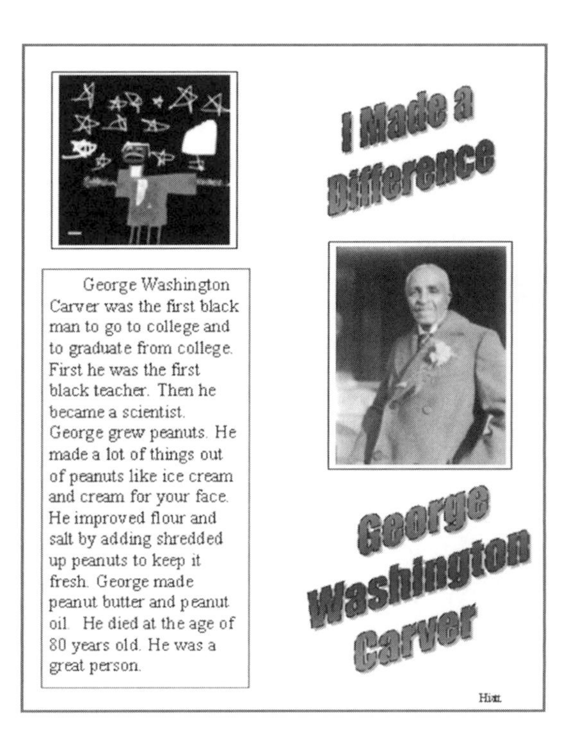

FIGURE 10.2 Second-grader Hiatt read about George Washington Carver during a unit on people who made a difference. Carver's many accomplishments inspired Hiatt to write an extensive paragraph.

Bookmarks, Style 2 (1–5)

A second bookmark style calls for dividing a landscape slide into four sections, with the middle sections each being .25 inches larger than the end sections. Placing three light but thick lines to separate the columns helps students know where each section ends. Once a slide template has been designed, the teacher can insert a duplicate slide for the reverse side of the bookmark.

Students design the front of the bookmark on slide 1 and copy and paste it to the remaining three sections of that slide. On slide 2, they design the reverse side and copy and paste it to fill in the second slide. The bookmarks can be printed two-sided as full-page slides on cardstock and cut into four bookmarks. The dividing lines can be removed before printing.

Bookmarks are particularly effective if students can exchange them with other students in the same grade level or leave them for the classroom library at the end of the year as motivators for the following year's students.

Money Practice (1–2)

To assess what students know about coin values, use a large four-cell table and place clip art of the standard coins (penny, nickel, dime, and quarter) at the top of the sheet. Teachers can give students specific instructions (i.e., in each box show a different way to make 25 cents) and quickly assess which students understand the various combinations that make the correct total. To complete this project, students learn to copy and paste the coins, a great skill to introduce and an authentic reason to use it.

Single Slides (2–5)

Single slides print with bright colors and fit nicely on a single sheet of paper. Students make single slides to use as cards (for Mother's Day, Thanksgiving, etc.), report covers, or classroom projects. While these could be done in word processing, students find presentation software easier to use. They also love adding background colors or pictures. Just as in any other program, in presentation software you can change the page orientation from landscape to portrait or choose custom sizes, so it can also be used in the same way that a word processing page can be used.

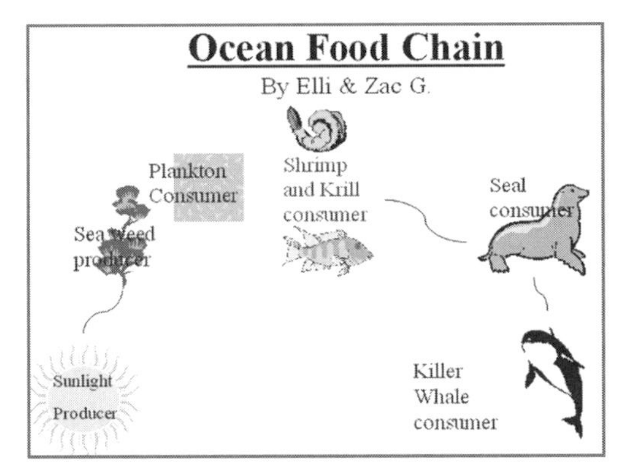

FIGURE 10.3 Third graders Elli and Zac teamed up to demonstrate their knowledge about the food chain in the ocean.

Class Shows (2–5)

Sometimes a teacher wants to capitalize on students' knowledge of presentation software but the project doesn't warrant the time or depth of information for every student to make a separate show. That's when each student can make one slide and contribute it to a class show.

Students research items related to an historic theme, such as Civil War issues, American presidents, or space exploration. Each student then creates a single slide with key words or phrases and photographs based on his/her research. The slides are imported into master slide shows and organized by some criteria (i.e., chronology, contrasting arguments, etc.). Students then present the material to peers or parents with each student speaking about one slide. Fourth-grade students sometimes use this method for teaching one another about space exploration, a topic on which they have little background knowledge.

Some second-grade classes develop slide shows in which each student contributes personal mottos and tips for being successful in second grade. The teachers save these slide shows for presentation to the following year's class of new students.

Teachers have asked students to make ABC lists or slide shows to capture key ideas of curricular units. Sometimes each student generates his own, but in many cases either small groups of students or the whole class will develop an ABC slide show. One fifth-grade teacher uses these for review at the end of the unit.

Photo Albums (2–5)

Photo albums have become a popular way to share context or extra photos with others. When students take photos on field trips, they make captioned photo pages to share with their parents. Photo album pages created in portrait layout fit easily into three-ring binders.

Second graders make photo albums as part of their slide shows on people who have made a difference. Some students use only pictures, but others add original illustrations.

When fourth-grade students learn about the famous people of Colorado, the primary assignment is to develop a biographic monologue as though they were the person. Students dress in costume and present their speeches to parents. In the process of researching their characters, they enjoy seeing historic photos of places, events, and people referenced in their speeches. They now create electronic photo albums with captioned pictures of these people and places. In some classes the photo albums are projected as accompaniment to the speeches.

Autoshapes in the Drawing Toolbar

Most drawing toolbars provide some version of shapes that can be inserted on pages. These shapes may be speech bubbles, lines and arrows, geometric shapes such as circles and rectangles, and irregular shapes. When students learn how to use the shapes, they invent many purposes for adding shapes to documents.

Speech and thought bubbles can be added to clip art or photographs to build cartoons. Arrows and lines can direct the reader to side notes or can pinpoint a location on a map. Students love to use shapes as backgrounds for their titles and captions.

As an alternative to commercial software, shapes enable students to create Webs and timelines. If the drawing toolbar also provides connectors, students can even link two shapes together so that if they have to be rearranged on the page, they won't unlink.

Since shapes can be filled with colors or special effects, students have options for adding color as background for text. As the photo album shows, students can insert a picture as the background for a shape and make the picture look as though it is framed.

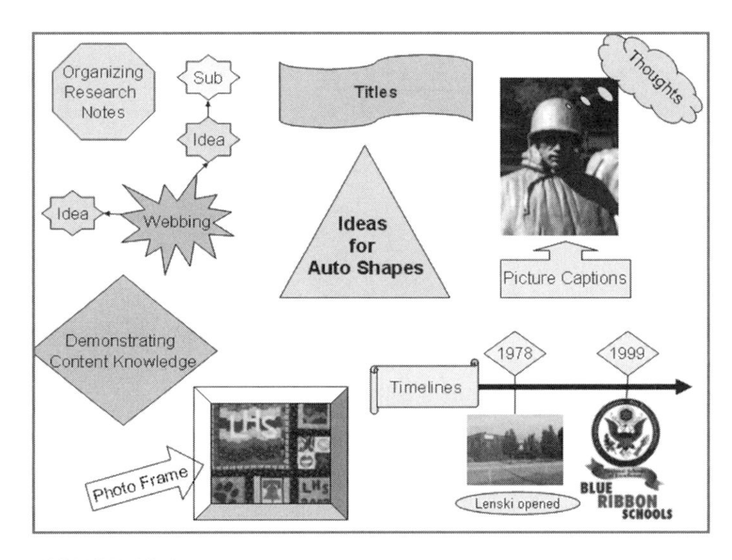

FIGURE 10.4 The author created this slide in PowerPoint to demonstrate how Autoshapes can enhance slides. Shapes can be used in most, if not all, productivity software applications.

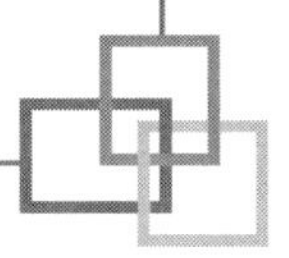

Growth Cycles (2–5)

With drawing software, students create series of pictures demonstrating growth cycles, such as plants from seeds to blooms (See chapter 6). Students then import the pictures into slide shows and add timed transitions so that the slides advance every three seconds. The slide shows resemble stop-action video. These slide shows make great public relations tools during parent-teacher conferences. When parents can watch a slide show while they wait for their appointments, they aren't as impatient if the preceding conference goes overtime.

Acrostics (2–5)

Presentation software has become the school's favorite medium for acrostics in recent years because of its flexibility, including the ability to lay out the page in portrait or landscape. For students who have short key words to incorporate, landscape orientation may be preferable while longer key words work better in portrait orientation. Students can use vertical WordArt to add their key word(s) to the screen and stretch the term(s) to fill the entire page. It's easy to move the WordArt around on the page as well.

To add the remaining text of the acrostic, students simply draw text boxes and type in the boxes. We teach them to double-click on the text box tool so the tool stays selected until they off-click it. This is a rapid way to add boxes. If the text doesn't line up with the major letter, students can easily move the boxes. Students can add clip art or pictures as well as background colors, if they desire.

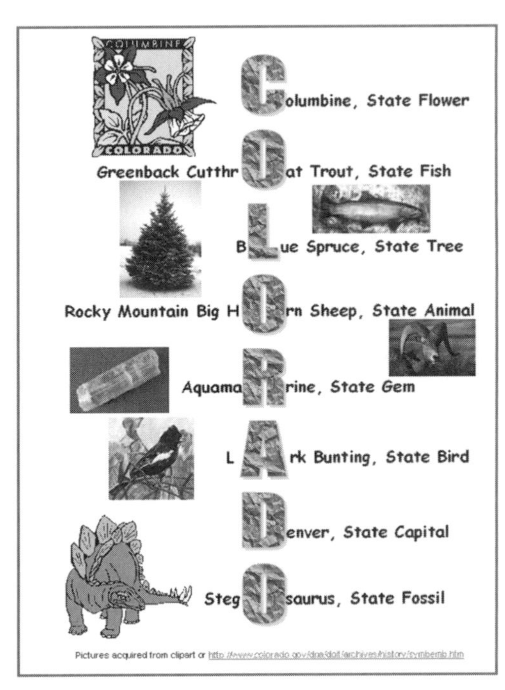

FIGURE 10.5 As this author-created acrostic shows, the letters of the key word may come at the beginning or middle of the word or phrase. Although the project was completed in presentation software, when printed, it looks like any word-processed document.

Acrostic Displays as an Instructional Choice

Acrostics allow students to demonstrate what they know about a subject in a graphically pleasing way—if a teacher sets the proper expectations. In an acrostic, students use large colorful letters to write the primary word, such as AUTUMN, vertically. The remaining letters are written horizontally in smaller, standard type. Although, traditionally, the letters of the primary word begin each line of the acrostic, students may use a word or phrase where the letter of the primary word ends up within the line. In an acrostic on autumn, for instance, the first line might be 'Apples, red and crisp' but the second line might be "leaves rUstling in the wind." Depending on the age level and ability of the student, a teacher may opt for single descriptive words for each letter or phrases.

The following examples show the difference a teacher might expect for an acrostic on DESERT depending on the age and ability of the students.

Dry
Empty
Sand
Extremely hot
Rocks
Treeless

Diverse animal and plant life (second to rainforest)
Extreme dryness and temperatures (hot or cold desert)
Survival depends on adaptation to conserve water
Extreme evaporation in windstorms
Rain of 10 inches or less a year
Temperatures swing 50°–60° between day and night

The teacher needs to set high expectations for any acrostic. The first acrostic above would be an excellent first- or second-grade project because it requires only one word per letter. A third or fourth grader who has researched deserts for a week or more should be able to include details similar to the second sample. Setting high expectations means the teacher also must provide sufficient time for students to find the factual material and wrestle with phrasings to incorporate the primary letters.

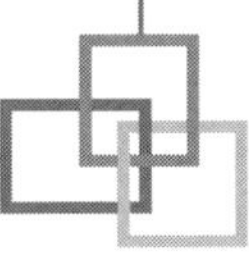

Postcards (2–5)

With postcards, students need to write tightly in order to fit the most important information on the card. They also write from the perspective of another person, so they use their imagination, fueled by what they've learned about the topic. The finished products give the teacher insight into the concepts of the units that stuck with the students and any glaring holes in understanding.

Teachers can fit a postcard into almost any science or social studies unit. In the role of a famous scientist, a student can speculate on how a discovery will impact the future. Students studying rocks and minerals can write as though they were geologists evaluating a sample submitted by a member of the public. In social studies, students can take on the perspective of any person in history to write about family life, government, wars, or journeys. Third-grade students write in the role of immigrants letting their families know what to expect at Ellis Island when they arrive in the United States.

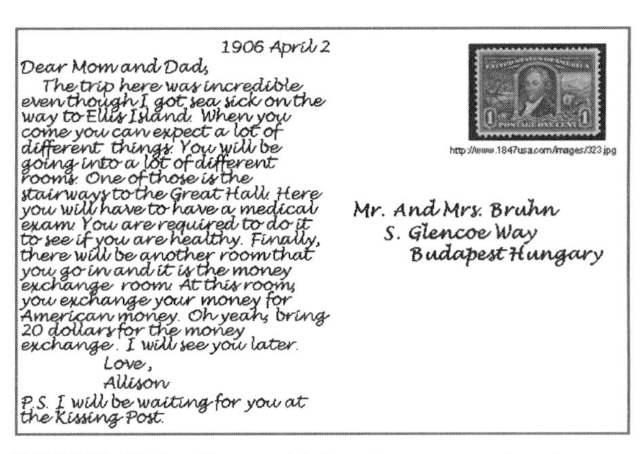
1906 April 2

Dear Mom and Dad,

The trip here was incredible even though I got sea sick on the way to Ellis Island. When you come you can expect a lot of different things. You will be going into a lot of different rooms. One of those is the stairways to the Great Hall. Here you will have to have a medical exam. You are required to do it to see if you are healthy. Finally, there will be another room that you go in and it is the money exchange room. At this room, you exchange your money for American money. Oh yeah, bring 20 dollars for the money exchange. I will see you later.

Love,

Allison

P.S. I will be waiting for you at the Kissing Post.

http://www.1847usa.com/images/323.jpg

Mr. And Mrs. Bruhn
S. Glencoe Way
Budapest Hungary

FIGURE 10.6 Allison, a third grader, wrote as though she had recently gone through the immigration process in 1906 and was preparing her parents to follow her. Notice that she included the Web site for the stamp.

Although students have successfully made postcards using word processors in the past, the switch to presentation software has removed obstacles encountered in word processing, particularly the need to format pictures and textboxes. As the sample shows, the slide is set up in portrait orientation and divided horizontally. Students place the message, address and stamp on the top portion and a picture on the bottom. The second slide has those elements in reverse order so that the slides can be printed two-sided and cut apart for two single postcards.

Trading Cards (2–5)

In presentation software, a person can turn on a grid that divides the page evenly into four sections or, if that option is missing, use two bisecting lines to split the screen. This becomes a template for trading cards, whether the presentation screen is landscape or portrait. Avery makes perforated card stock for postcards, but teachers could also choose to use thick paper and cut it into fourths after printing.

Students create trading cards to share what they've learned with others. In second grade, for instance, students research children's authors and read books by the author they've studied. In computer lab, they create trading cards about their authors. On one side, they identify the author and, when possible, include a photograph of the author. On the reverse side, they write about a favorite book by that author. Their intent is to convince classmates to read their authors' books. When printed, the sheet provides one card for the teacher, one to take home and two to trade with classmates. Often the teachers place their copies at the classroom library as a resource when students they are searching for a book.

Students make postcards for famous astronomers, fact cards about planets, and notecards highlighting events that influenced American history. The postcards can even be used for riddles. Students write clues about something they've researched (planets, volcanoes, continents, famous people) on one side of the card. On the reverse, they give the answer and illustrate with an original drawing. Technology teachers can create postcard cheat sheets with directions for common tasks teachers or students may do in productivity software. At one time, we collected postcards
with instructions on how to insert pictures, make tables, and do other tasks onto an O-ring and hung the rings on the sides of teachers' monitors. This helped teachers feel safe if they asked students to work on a project and the students had questions.

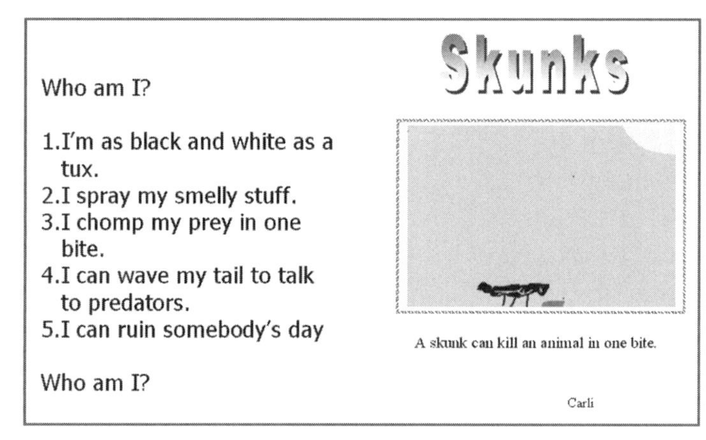

FIGURE 10.7 Carli, a third grader, researched skunks during a unit on animal habitats and adaptations. On one side she wrote clues, facts that make the animal unique but aren't too obvious. On the other side, she put the answer, a drawing of the animal and the most amazing fact she learned.

Group Projects (2–5)

Students work in teams to research a complex topic and distill the information for their peers. Together they create a multi-slide presentation where each student researches and illustrates one aspect. A slide show on the Bill of Rights, where students use clip art or personal drawings with call-outs, such as speech bubbles, to cartoon the central ideas, can be memorable both for the students involved in the project and for their audience. Ideas for team slide shows include regions of the country, continents, geometric forms (finding examples of geometric shapes in everyday life), and simple machines.

Dictionaries and Collections (2–5)

Creating a vocabulary or idiom dictionary makes vocabulary a visual activity. At Lenski, students participate in Dictionary Day. On that day, students dress up to illustrate a word they've pre-selected with teacher approval. Each child has his photo taken. In the lab, students create one-page documents with the pertinent information about their words: pronunciation, part of speech, meaning, synonyms and antonyms, sample sentences and, of course, their pictures. These one-page documents are alphabetized in notebooks and placed in classrooms. Months later, students still remember the words in the Dictionary Day notebooks.

paraphernalia

(noun)

-gear; personal belongings or equipment

We had to bring a lot of sports paraphernalia to the baseball tournament.

FIGURE 10.8 Lenski's fifth graders participate in Dictionary Day twice a year. Students dress as nonlinguistic representations of words. They share their words multiple times with other student groups and have their pictures taken. In the following week, students create standardized dictionary pages and print copies for all fifth-grade classrooms. When students come across the words in their reading, even months later, they remember what the words mean and who dressed up to depict them.

Similarly, students illustrate common idioms. This idea grew out of the realization that students often miss nuances in their reading because they don't recognize idioms. Students visit ESL (English as a Second Language) Web sites to choose idioms and illustrate their choices through the use of clip art and/or drawings. These are collected into idiom dictionaries.

Other collections may include vocabulary specific to a content area, such as geography or parts of the sentence. Dictionary collections can be shared with other classes or the dictionary pages can be displayed in a hallway so that students in other classes can benefit.

RESOURCES

Idiom Websites

While teachers can probably think of many idioms that are used in everyday life, students often don't recognize idioms as idioms. If the idiomatic expressions are in their common vocabulary, students think everyone knows them. If the phrases are unfamiliar, the students are more likely to skip over them rather than look them up.

Idioms can be an excellent introduction to figurative language as well. Often idioms are metaphors or similes that have been shortened or have become so common they are now trite. But, when idioms first came to life, they were original ways to compare unlike things. A fun exercise for students can be to collect idiomatic expressions that have not yet become common or to create their own.

UsingEnglish.com (www.usingenglish.com/reference/idioms/): UsingEnglish.com began in 2002 and offers free memberships to access all the ESL materials. The idiom dictionary available to all non-members has 72 idioms; the member dictionary has more than 1,500 entries. The entries are alphabetized and include the idiom and a brief explanation. Much of the site is geared toward British English speakers, although many of the idioms are recognizable in the United States.

The Idiom Connection (www.idiomconnection.com/): This site has been around since 1997 and has an extensive list of idioms that can be accessed alphabetically or by category. Individual listings include the idiom, the meaning, and a sentence using the idiom.

English Daily (www.englishdaily626.com/idioms.php): For each idiom, this site gives a short dialogue with the idiom in context and a response that gives the definition. The site has only 44 idioms, but the entries are good examples of how idioms infiltrate speech.

Go English (www.goenglish.com/Idioms.asp): Go English lists a number of popular idioms with sentences that explain the meanings of the idioms in context. Each idiom is hyperlinked to a separate window with a more thorough explanation of the idiom with additional examples and a cartoon of the idiomatic expression.

Trifold Brochures (2–5)

Brochures seem as though they should be easy for students to create because the sections are narrow, but the need to fill six sections with different kinds of information requires that students study their topics in depth. Generally, students will build brochures after research units because they have a wealth of knowledge by the time they finish taking notes. We encourage them to write quizzes, build graphs, and make bulleted lists for different sections of the brochures so that the space is easily filled without dense text. Decorative clip art related to their topics also helps fill space.

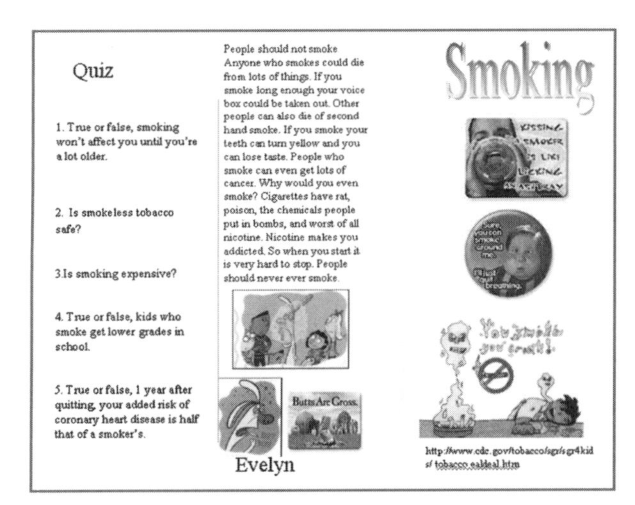

FIGURE 10.9 Evelyn researched the effects of smoking as part of a fifth-grade unit on the respiratory system. She created a brochure to educate other students.

Similar to the bookmarks, the template for a brochure in presentation software has thick lines where the creases will go. Because slides have a half-inch margin built in, the center section needs to be half an inch larger than either side (3.7 rather than 3.2 inches). When the first slide is finished, inserting a duplicate slide will keep the creases in the right place. Small text boxes can identify what type of information goes into each section, such as title, bibliography, pictures, etc. The number of text boxes depends on the level and abilities of students. The thick colored lines serve as margins for each section. Just before printing, students delete the lines.

When second graders research foreign countries, they advertise for tourists through brochures. Third graders sometimes use brochures to market trips to the planets they study, and fourth graders generate brochures about the U.S. regions. As part of a health unit on fitness, students choose topics such as the dangers of drug and cigarette use or the benefits of healthy eating for their brochures. They often place their brochures in book pockets attached to a bulletin board in the hallway. This way students from other grade levels can read the brochures.

Modeling Non-fiction Text Elements (4–5)

Teachers sometimes find it difficult to get students to demonstrate that they understand the text elements of a non-fiction book. Slide shows can incorporate the elements of expository text, such as title pages, tables of contents, glossaries, bibliographies, and indices.

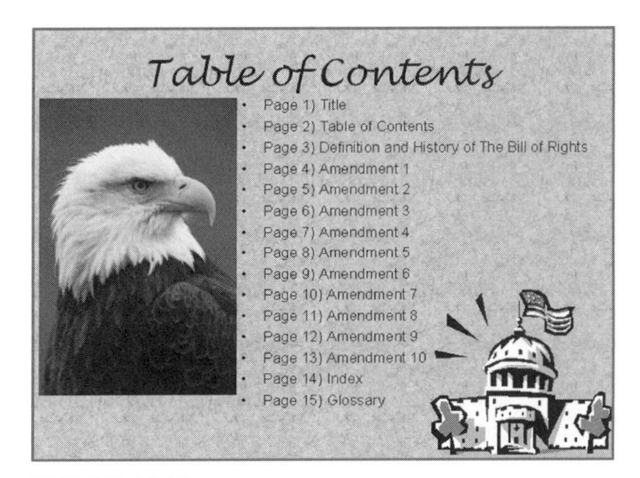

FIGURE 10.10 This teacher sample replicates the typical fifth grader's table of contents for a presentation on the Bill of Rights. Note that the table of contents refers to an index and a glossary on slides 14 and 15.

Homophones (4–5)

Learning to discriminate between two words that sound alike but have different spellings and meanings (homophones) poses a huge challenge to many students. If they create visual vocabulary pages to attach pictures to the words, some students will remember the differences better. One fifth-grade teacher not only has students create a homophone book for their classroom, but posts copies of the homophone pages on a bulletin board in the hall to help other students remember the differences.

FIGURE 10.11 Fifth-grader Kelly chose a homophone with three spellings. She inserted clip art and wrote sentences to illustrate the differences among the words.

Character Webs (4–5)

To reinforce the techniques for developing three-dimensional characters in a story, one fifth grade teacher asks students to complete character webs. In the center oval, students write three traits that define their characters. They make each trait its own color.

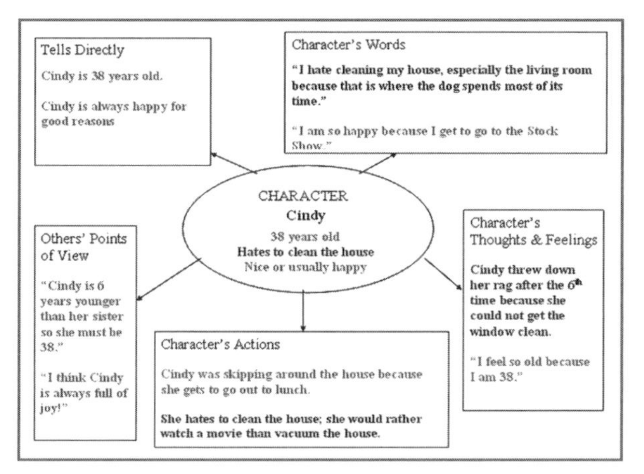

FIGURE 10.12 Megan, a fifth grader, chose an adult female as her character for the web. By writing details about how she would characterize Cindy in a story, she gave herself an outline for making Cindy a well-rounded character in a story.

In the surrounding shapes, they write ways that the character's traits could be revealed to readers and color-code them to match the traits in the center oval. When students then write their stories, they include the details and dialogue from their webs. This same strategy can be used to analyze a character during the study of a novel in reading class.

Visual Poetry (4–5)

Creating visual poetry requires students to use their imaginations and technical skills with decorative text. Generally Lenski students can manage the technical skills, but the quality of the visual poems differs greatly from student to student because not all students have good visual imaginations.

Students first think of a concept they could convey through both the choice and placement of words. They then use decorative text to write the words so that the text illustrates the sense of the words.

FIGURE 10.13 Fifth-grader Nate combined clip art, decorative text, and a figure drawn in a drawing program to capture the movement and excitement of a soccer game as a visual poem.

Hyperlinked Shows (5)

Presentation software lends itself to hyperlinking from one slide to another. This turns a typically linear presentation into an interactive module. In this model, one slide becomes the master, perhaps a map or a table of contents. When the user clicks on hyperlinked text (the familiar blue underlined text as on Web sites), the show jumps to one or more slides on the specific topic. A button on the final slide of that topic returns the viewer to the master slide.

This use of hyperlinks works well for "museum" displays or any settings where people may independently want to explore presentations. Since such shows are often accessed independently and are not part of oral reports, the slides require more text than students typically use. Students hyperlink to Web sites, word-processed documents, or spreadsheets as easily as other slides.

Like the timed slide shows, hyperlinked slide shows can be used as exhibits during parent-teacher conferences. Parents can click on the links to their children's slides or explore several links.

Presentation software is so versatile and easy to use that teachers try projects first in slide shows rather than other applications. Students learn the tools quickly and enjoy the option of adding colored backgrounds to their work. Best of all, during curriculum nights and parent-teacher conferences, slide shows dynamically demonstrate to parents what students are learning.

LESSON PLAN

Grade 1, Using Description

Teachers(s):	Collaborative Partner(s):
First Grade	Technology Teacher
Curricular Area(s):	Content Target(s):
Language Arts	Use descriptive words in writing

Standards Addressed:

National Language Arts Standards:

5. Using a range of strategies to communicate

ISTE National Technology Standards:

2. Using technology tools to enhance learning and promote creativity

Final Product:

- Students will describe pictures with colorful words and phrases.

Necessary Skills (Content, Technology, Information Literacy):

Content:

- Knowledge of adjectives and verbs; knowledge of how colorful language paints a picture

Technology:

- Typing into a slide, saving

TIMELINE:

DATE:	PERSON RESPONSIBLE:	ACTIVITY:
PRIOR TO DAY 1	Technology and Classroom Teachers	Collaborate on creating a slide show with seven to ten pictures, one per slide, and space for students to write their describing words. Save the template to a common location.
DAY 1	Classroom Teacher	Using literature, teacher introduces the concept of using precise words to paint pictures for readers. Students will generate lists of words that authors use to create visual images.
DAY 2	Technology or Classroom Teacher	Introduce students to the template. Guide them as they save copies into their folders. Demonstrate how to type into the text boxes.
	Classroom Teacher	Allot sufficient time for students to work in pairs on their describing words. When students finish, they add their names and print two copies with four to six slides per page for their portfolios or writing notebooks.

FIGURE 10.14 Working in pairs, students come up with as many descriptive words and phrases as they can. The slide show should have pictures that cover a range of textures, feelings, colors, and activities so that students don't use the same words for two slides.

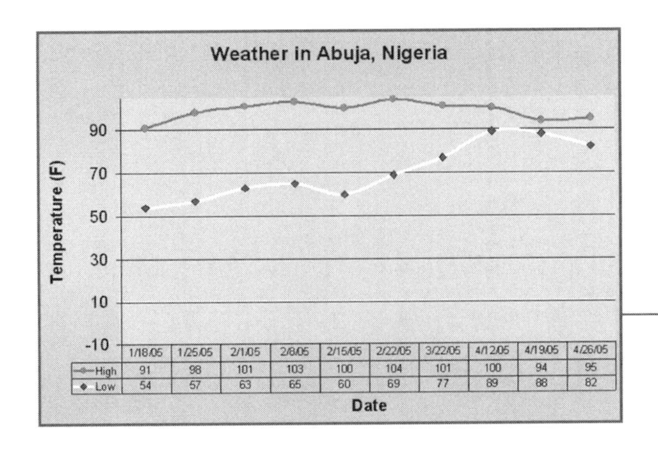

	1/18/05	1/25/05	2/1/05	2/8/05	2/15/05	2/22/05	3/22/05	4/12/05	4/19/05	4/26/05
High	91	98	101	103	100	104	101	100	94	95
Low	54	57	63	65	60	69	77	89	88	82

Chapter 11

Databases and Spreadsheets

OF ALL THE PRODUCTIVITY SOFTWARE TOOLS AVAILABLE TO TEACHERS, databases and spreadsheets receive the least attention and use. In fact, some would question whether these two tools are appropriate for elementary students. However, I believe that both applications have appropriate places in the elementary curriculum.

While generally elementary students do not need to learn how to create databases, they do need to be proficient in the use of databases as tools for retrieving information. Even early elementary students can create Boolean searches for computerized library catalogs. Intermediate students should learn basic searching skills for online databases, including popular search engines.

The basics of spreadsheets can be introduced in early elementary and more advanced skills added later. Graphing and the use of data sets support data analysis and probability instruction; the use of simple formulas supports algebra. Other spreadsheet tools work similarly to tools in word processing and presentation applications.

Databases

Databases may be simple, such as one table and a form for entering data, or complex, such as a set of tables with unique identifiers and defined relationships among the tables. Simple databases were popular in the early 90s, particularly for Apple computer owners, but have lost their appeal because word processing and spreadsheet programs can now accomplish comparable tasks. Complex databases, called relational databases, require advanced skills in design and organization that exceed what elementary students can handle.

On the other hand, students can and should learn to *use* databases. Automated library records and Web search engines are two examples of databases students can learn to use effectively. Other relational databases in schools, generally used only by staff, include student information systems, gradebooks, and bookkeeping records.

Traditionally, librarians have taught students how to search for and use reference materials. Teachers could bask in the knowledge that not only were students learning reference skills in the library but the materials they were using had been pre-screened by an editor and the purchaser. Today, not only do many elementary schools lack trained librarians, but students access a wide range of online materials that may not have been pre-screened and may, in fact, be inaccurate or biased. More than ever, students need to learn skills for selecting, evaluating, and citing resources. To ignore these essential skills places children at grave risk.

At Lenski, appropriately accessing online databases and using search engines effectively are taught as part of research projects in both the library and computer lab. Schools that lack professionals in those instructional areas need to identify when and how these skills will be taught.

Spreadsheets

Spreadsheets fit into elementary school programs well. Although most adults think of spreadsheets as purely financial tools, students can use the software for other purposes. Many teachers, including computer teachers, are unfamiliar with spreadsheets, so they tend to avoid using spreadsheets with students. However, a little time spent on the computer poking around in a spreadsheet application may unveil hidden potential for student use.

RESOURCES

Information Literacy Resources

As part of 21st-century learning, students need to learn information literacy skills through classroom activities. The Web offers a number of resources to support the integration of information literacy with classroom instruction.

FREE INFORMATION LITERACY LESSONS

- **21st Century Literacies** (www.kn.att.com/wired/21stcent/gradelevel.html): The Lesson Grade Level Chart on this site was created to support the *AT&T/UCLA Initiative for the 21st Century Literacies*, links to model lessons and indicates grade-level appropriateness for students. Many lessons cover more than one grade-level grouping.
- **Searching the Net** (www.teachingideas.co.uk/welcome/searching/index.htm): The large text size and simple design of this British site make it a friendly practice area for older elementary students. Each page covers one concept of Web searching and students do activities within the site to practice proper search techniques and learn the pitfalls.

FREE CITATION TOOLS

- **Landmark's Son of Citation Machine** (http://citationmachine.net): Students may use the tools of this Web site to create citations for their bibliographies. This Web site creates bibliographic records for both print and non-print sources in either MLA or APA style.
- **NoodleTools** (www.noodletools.com): The NoodleBib MLA Starter is a free MLA citation tool for students in grades 1–6. Students can copy and paste bibliography records directly from NoodleTools into the application they are using for their projects. Students have to register before they begin to use the site. More extensive tools are available through subscriptions.
- **KnightCite** (http://Webapps.calvin.edu/knightcite/): Provided by the Heckman Library at Calvin College, this site provides only citation services. The site is free and very simple to use. Students choose the style of citation and the type of reference source. The final citation does not attempt to capitalize titles correctly because of the many variables, but clear instructions below the citation give the guidelines for capitalization according to the style of citation. All citations for this book were created at KnightCite.

Acrostics (2–5)

As explained in the previous chapter, acrostics may be created in almost any application. Some teachers prefer word processing software; some prefer presentation software; and others use spreadsheets.

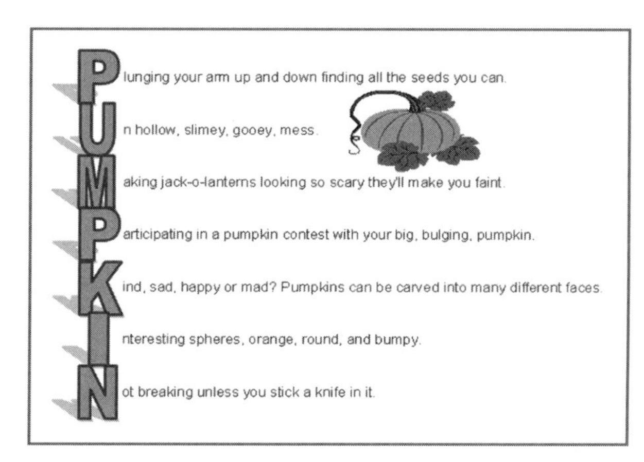

FIGURE 11.1 In his pumpkin acrostic, third grader Dallin tried to convey images of carving a pumpkin through word choice. This acrostic has the look and feel of a poem.

In a spreadsheet application, students need to do some preliminary work before they add their words. Students make columns A and C wider to accommodate their wording. Set column A to right justification and column C to left justification.

Students write their key word in decorative font that is three cells high in column B. (One method for this is to have students write their first letters in decorative font, such as WordArt, move it into column B and resize it until it is three cells high. Then copy and paste that letter as many times as there are letters in the primary word. For autumn, a student would size the A properly and then copy and paste the A five times. The copied letter will paste wherever the cursor sits, so it makes sense to put the cursor in column B each time. Double-clicking on the letter will let the student change the letter from A to the correct letter. Using this process makes all the letters the same size and appearance.)

Students then enter their text in columns A and/or C, beside the oversized letters of their key word. They can choose whether they prefer the additional text in the middle or third row of each primary letter. When the text has all been entered, students should look at a print preview to see how the text fits on the page. To make it fit the page better, select the entire page and change the font size to be either larger or smaller. Students can then add clip art or photographs to decorate the page. When printed, the lines of the spreadsheet do not show.

Graphing (2–5)

Since data analysis appears on state testing, students benefit greatly when they create and interpret their own data tables and graphs. Fortunately, many curricular topics lend themselves to data analysis and spreadsheet practice.

One fifth-grade teacher asks her students to track all the books they read by genre. Each trimester, students graph their reading accomplishments and set goals for the following trimester. Students take pride in meeting and exceeding their goals, and by the end of the year, they have read a variety of genres they may never have tried otherwise.

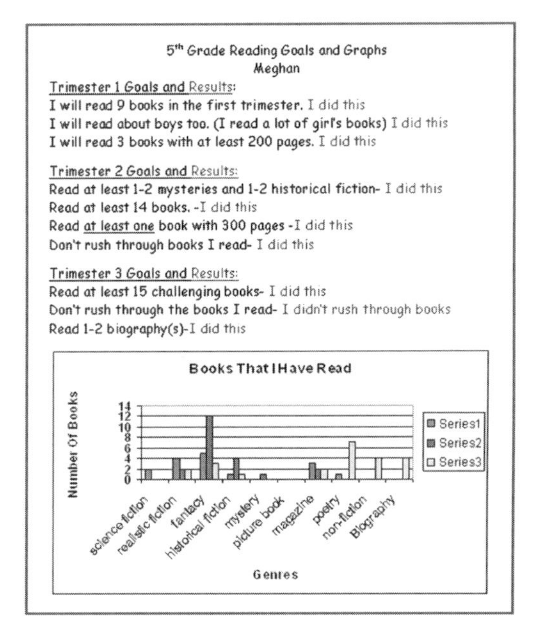

5th Grade Reading Goals and Graphs
Meghan

Trimester 1 Goals and Results:
I will read 9 books in the first trimester. I did this
I will read about boys too. (I read a lot of girl's books) I did this
I will read 3 books with at least 200 pages. I did this

Trimester 2 Goals and Results:
Read at least 1-2 mysteries and 1-2 historical fiction- I did this
Read at least 14 books. -I did this
Read at least one book with 300 pages -I did this
Don't rush through books I read- I did this

Trimester 3 Goals and Results:
Read at least 15 challenging books- I did this
Don't rush through the books I read- I didn't rush through books
Read 1-2 biography(s)-I did this

FIGURE 11.2 Meghan, a fifth grader, increased the number of books she read as well as sampling different genres during the school year. Graphing book choices highlights areas for growth and makes students accountable for goals they set.

Another group of fifth graders brainstorm their questions about middle school, develop a survey, send it to a middle school, and graph the responses. What a powerful way to prepare students to transition to the next level!

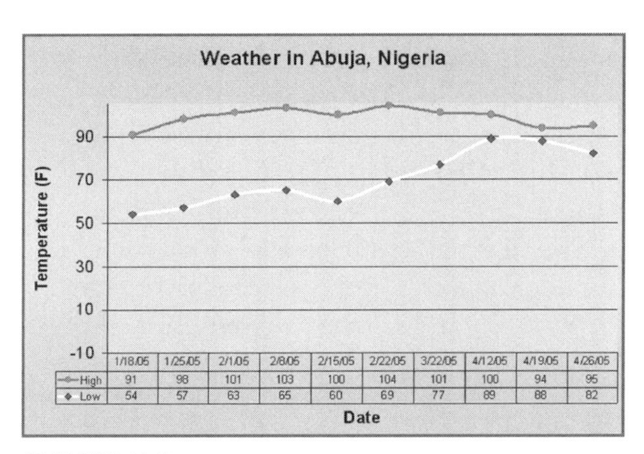

	1/18/05	1/25/05	2/1/05	2/8/05	2/15/05	2/22/05	3/22/05	4/12/05	4/19/05	4/26/05
High	91	98	101	103	100	104	101	100	94	95
Low	54	57	63	65	60	69	77	89	88	82

FIGURE 11.3 Second grader Courtney graphed the high and low temperatures in Abuja, Nigeria, from January 18, 2005 through April 26, 2005. She visited http://weather.yahoo.com weekly during computer lab to gather the data. However, she did not have enough data to know whether the diminishing gap between the high and low temperatures in April was typical or whether the temperatures represented an unusual weather pattern. With one temperature a week and only three to four months of data, students sometimes ended up with graphs skewed by unusual weather. Often the inferences students made were inaccurate because of the limited data.

Second graders struggle to grasp the abstract concepts of weather because they assume weather is the same everywhere. For several years, during their country research, we had them track the temperature highs and lows in their research countries' capitals in spreadsheets. At the end of the study, they would graph the temperatures and try to determine the season of year. However, at best, they ended up with two months of data, not enough to make good inferences. Now we have them record the monthly high and low temperatures for their capital as well as for Denver for twelve months. When they graph both sets of numbers, they end up with clear comparisons, which always yield surprises. They don't

RESOURCES

Weather Resources

To find the average high and low temperatures and/or precipitation for locations around the world, try any of these Web sites:

World Climate (www.worldclimate.com): The home page of World Climate has all the vital information about how to use the site. Historical data is organized under the name the country used on the date the temperature was recorded, which would be an interesting lesson in itself. To start the search, enter a city name or click on a major city name.

Weather.com (www.weather.com/common/home/climatology.html): Enter a city name; for Lisbon, it offered multiple cities around the world, not just Portugal. The site also offers record highs and lows for each location.

WeatherBase (www.weatherbase.com): This site has comprehensive data on over 16,000 cities worldwide. Set the data unit preference to either U.S. or Metric before you search. Choose a country or part of the world, or search for a city, country, or zip code.

expect Denver to have some hotter months than cities near the equator or northern Canada to be quite so cold. When asked to contrast and compare the graphs, they are able to make more accurate inferences. In the future, the teachers plan to allow enough time for students to compare the monthly precipitation as well.

By default, spreadsheet graphs automatically display data according to the range of numbers in the data table. So, a student tracking weather in Toronto may have a temperature range between -20° and 80°, while a classmate studying a country on the equator may log temperatures between 60° and 110°. Unless they adjust the ranges of their graphs to be identical, they may think their countries have similar climates because the graph lines look similar. Within a class, all students should set their scales to be the same, representing the highest and lowest temperatures recorded. That way, they will be able to compare their graphs and see the differences in climate.

When students finish their graphs, they need to interpret the results. Options include importing the graphs to presentation or word processing software so that they can write conclusions, printing the graphs and hand-writing the conclusions on the graphs, or posting all the graphs and discussing the differences as a class.

Webbing and Timelines (2–5)

Similar to presentation software, spreadsheet software has drawing capabilities. First, students need to select the entire page and fill with white, sort of like painting the page white. Students can use a combination of AutoShapes, Connectors, clip art, and pictures to create Webs and timelines. Since spreadsheets can cover multiple pages that can then be taped together, students have unlimited space for their Webs and timelines.

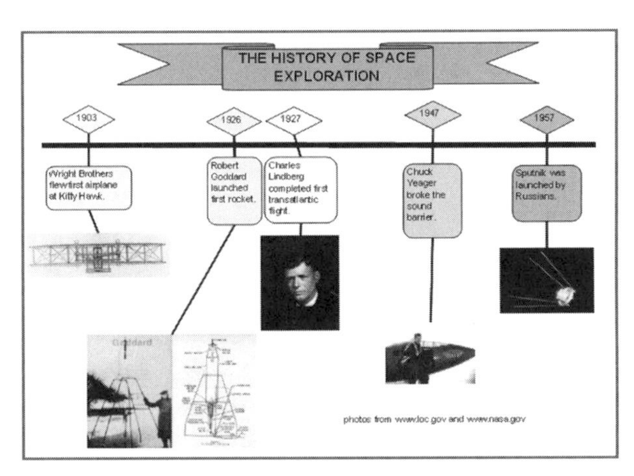

FIGURE 11.4 This teacher-created sample shows the major events of space exploration. Timelines in a spreadsheet have unlimited boundaries, because a student can print many pages and connect them.

Money Management (4–5)

Many money managers use spreadsheets, so it's natural to teach students to track income and expenses through spreadsheets. Although this may be more comfortable at middle and high school, elementary teachers can expose students to the potential of spreadsheets as management tools.

Lenski's advanced math students do a math extension project titled "If I Had a Million...," where they develop a plan for spending a million dollars. They can enter their spending in a spreadsheet, where a simple formula can track the total expenditures.

Student Leadership operates a store at Lenski and tries to track their expenses and sales through a simple spreadsheet. They need support in setting up the spreadsheet, but keeping it current is not a difficult task for the treasurer.

An introduction to databases and spreadsheets in elementary school prepares students for more sophisticated work in middle school. Certainly, students need explicit instruction on the use of databases so that they can be successful on independent research projects as they advance through school. The use of spreadsheets reinforces math skills in data management, graph analysis, and number sense. Introducing spreadsheets at the elementary level makes students aware of computer tools that they can explore in greater depth as they mature.

LESSON PLAN

Grade 5, Middle School Survey

Teachers(s):	Collaborative Partner(s):
Fifth Grade	Technology Teacher
Curricular Area(s):	**Content Target(s):**
Math	Collect and analyze data; construct graphs
Language Arts	Write survey questions

Standards Addressed:

National Math Standards:

5. Collecting and analyzing data
10. Creating graphs to communicate mathematical ideas

National Language Arts Standards:

1. Reading for varied purposes
5. Communicating to audiences
8. Using the research process to gain information

ISTE National Technology Standards:

4. Using technology research tools to process data and communicate results
5. Using technology resources for making decisions

Final Product:

- Students will survey middle school students on questions related to entering middle school.
- Students will create graphs that communicate the results of their surveys.

Necessary Skills (Content, Technology, Information Literacy):

Content:

- Know how to create an effective question to garner appropriate results
- Know how to record data and graph it to be effective as a communications tool

Technology:

- Using a spreadsheet application for recording data and creating meaningful graphs

Timeline:

Dates	Person Responsible:	Activity:
Week 1	Classroom Teacher	Brainstorm with students about their concerns as they approach the transition to middle school. Teach questioning strategies. Place students in groups and assign the teams topics on which to develop questions. Provide opportunities for groups to work collaboratively to test their questions. Arrange with a middle school principal to distribute the surveys to sixth grade students in their homerooms and to collect the surveys at the end.
	Technology Teacher	Review with students how to set up a data table and graph data. Allow time for student teams to construct their data tables.
Week 2	Classroom Teacher	Allot time for students to enter their data and create graphs. Have students import their graphs into presentation slides and add conclusions based on the data. Provide time for a pair of students to insert all the slides into one show. Have teams present their findings to their fifth-grade peers.

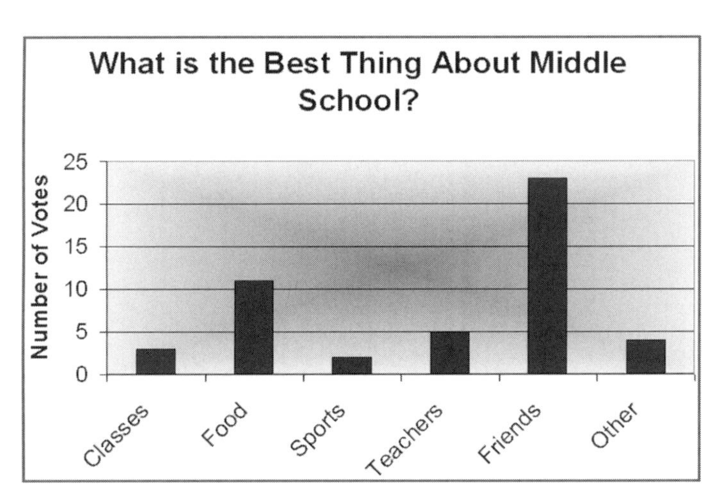

FIGURE 11.5 Lenski students were surprised at the results of the survey. They predicted students would rank friends and sports high. No one guessed that food would rank second in the survey. Most questions on the survey dealt with students' concerns about adjusting to middle school.

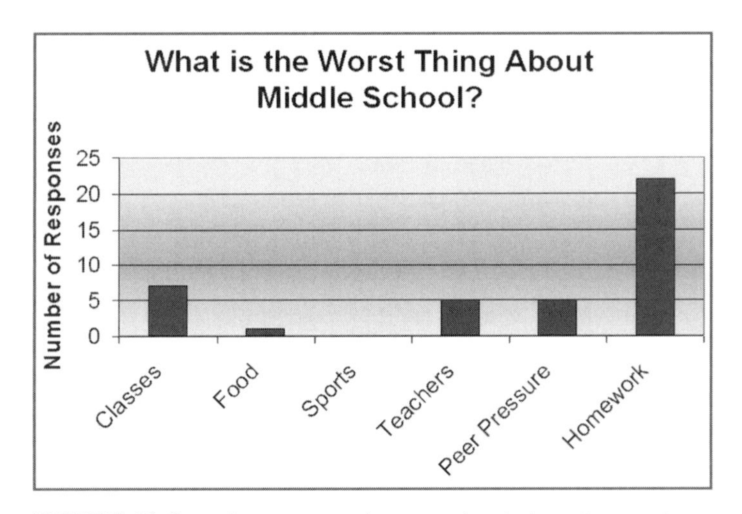

FIGURE 11.6 Students expressed concern that sixth graders rated homework as the worst part of middle school, but when they saw the results of the follow-up question about how long students spend on homework, they realized that most sixth graders spent 30–60 minutes on homework at night, the same length of time as the fifth graders spent. The survey results dispelled some concerns that fifth graders had. According to sixth graders, middle school students rarely get lost in the hallways or forget their locker combinations. Most important, sixth graders said that the upperclassmen did not pick on them or shove them into lockers.

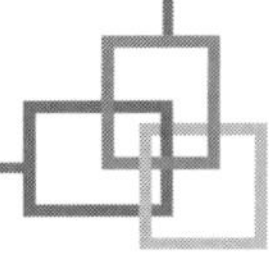

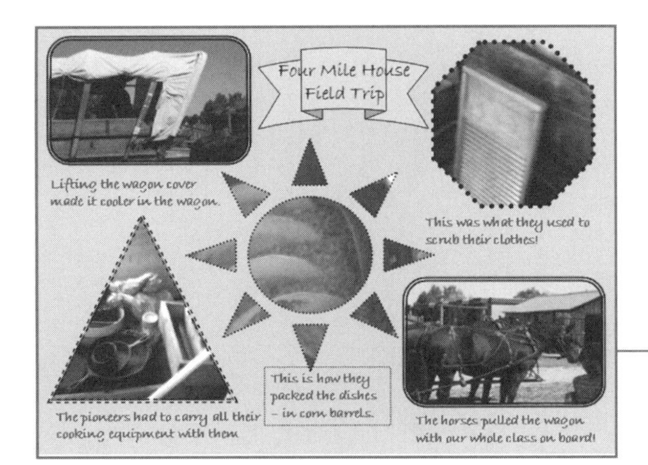

Chapter 12

Other Education Technologies

ALTHOUGH IT MAY BE POSSIBLE TO GET THROUGH A YEAR using only office productivity software, teachers have additional resources that can provide rich experiences for students.

INTERNET (K–5)

The number of free resources available on the Internet grows at an extraordinary rate, fast enough that no one can stay current. Fortunately, teachers can find lists of resources that link to some of the best Web sites. However, evaluating the sites may take hours, especially since each route reveals interesting side trails. One caveat: some sites are thinly disguised advertisements for television shows or commercial products, or are more entertainment than education. These may be fun for students, but if the educational content is not extremely high, keep looking. There are too many good resources to settle for a mediocre one.

Many sites make excellent activity centers for classrooms. After students are introduced to sites in a computer lab setting or through the use of a projection unit, the classroom teacher can then use the Web sites as activity centers without having to teach each student how to navigate them. Often these sites address basic reading and math skills such as alphabet order, phonics, number sense, and arithmetic operations. One excellent site for kindergarten and first grade students is Starfall.com.

Starfall (www.starfall.com) targets reading skills from pre-reading to emergent readers and the site adds more content regularly. They also offer inexpensively priced printed materials, which can be used with or without the Web site.

FIGURE 12.1 Starfall.com is a free online service that helps students learn to read.

For visual learners, virtual manipulatives reinforce math concepts extremely well. With virtual manipulatives, students get immediate feedback on their answers, so they don't continue to make the same mistakes. Virtual manipulatives are also neater, faster, and more efficient than concrete manipulatives. Concepts such as fractions, which many students find difficult, seem easier to understand using virtual manipulatives. Two useful manipulatives sites are the National Library of Virtual Manipulatives and Interactivate.

The **National Library of Virtual Manipulatives** (http://nlvm.usu.edu/en/nav/vlibrary.html) is maintained and updated by Utah State University staff under a grant from the National Science Foundation. Students through high school can use the manipulatives for visualizing math concepts and practicing math skills.

Interactivate (www.shodor.org/interactivate/elementary/index.html) started as a middle school manipulatives site, but has recently added an elementary-level page. In the activity above, students type input numbers to try to determine the mathematical rule being followed by the function machine.

Students need to develop logical thinking skills. Internet sites, including the virtual manipulative sites, sometimes offer problem-solving opportunities for students. After introducing these sites, teachers can encourage students to practice at home. One excellent site for logical thinking is zoopz.com.

Visitors to **Zoopz** (www.zoopz.com) can choose from several problem-solving activities. The Inch Worm, Inch Worm 2, and Frog Jumpin games require players to use logic to master progressively more difficult levels. The site doesn't save previous scores so allow plenty of time to get from Level 1 to the end. Elementary students in Grades 2 and higher can generally master 9–12 levels before they reach frustration.

FIGURE 12.2 Zoopz offers problem-solving as well as other fun educational activities.

Some sites are content-specific. Using interactive sites to practice language skills, to test students' understanding of simple machines, or to explore volcanoes can enrich the classroom experiences. First grades have studied insects through Internet collections of digital photographs. Third graders have tested their map skills through an interactive quiz. Fifth graders have practiced for hands-on dissections through virtual dissections.

Edheads (www.edheads.org) offers four interactive activities that fit into elementary curricula: Odd Machine, Virtual Knee Surgery, Weather, and Simple Machines. In the Simple Machines activity students search for ten simple machines in each of four rooms in a house. When they find each machine, they have to answer questions about the type of simple machine and its purpose. Allow 45–60 minutes for the entire activity, depending on students' prior knowledge about simple machines.

Instant Poetry Forms (http://ettcWeb.lr.k12.nj.us/forms/newpoem.htm) gives teachers many poetry form templates; such as description and detail, rhyme, and seasonal, for student work. Each poetry form gives instructions, a place to type and a sample poem. The Web site formats the poems in simple layouts, which can be printed.

Lenski students generally copy the poems and paste them into other software applications so that they can enhance the formatting.

Read·Write·Think (www.readwritethink.org/student_mat/) offers an extensive collection of interactive online tools to support literacy. Each student material module includes a link to the interactive tool and additional links to lesson plans using the tool.

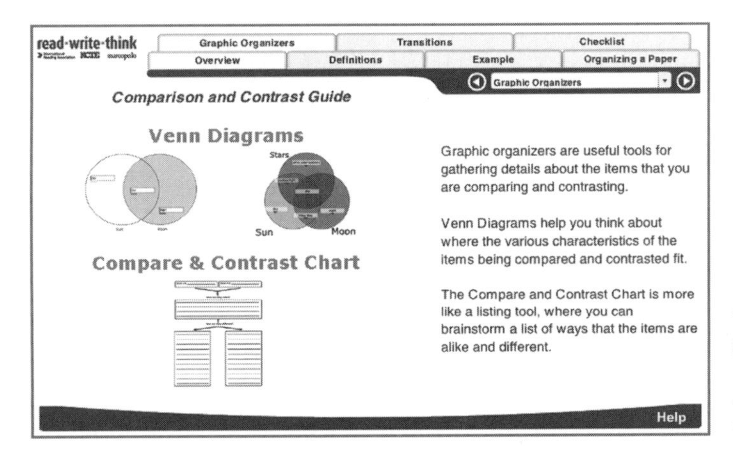

FIGURE 12.3 This screen shot comes from the interactive comparison and contrast guide module where students first learn about using graphic organizers to capture thoughts and then can choose the tool that suits their topic best.

Some states and testing services publish sample assessments in reading, writing, math and science. Teachers can use these for practice sessions or even as mini-assessments to evaluate where students may need more instruction.

Websites can also be used in non-traditional ways. Elementary students rarely have the abstract reasoning ability to grasp maps, but they generally have a sense of how long it takes to get to and from school. On a site like mapquest.com, have each student query for a map that goes from the school to home. The map will not only highlight the shortest route, but it will also calculate the distance and the time by car. Students can print out their maps and write clues to identify their maps. Their classmates can try to match the maps with the clues. This exercise has several benefits: students learn their home addresses (a skill many lack), they practice higher-level thinking skills in developing clues, and they learn about an Internet service that will help them as they grow up.

Don't pass up the opportunity to share good Web sites with parents. You can make it easier for parents to guide their children to good sites if you publish two to four sites a month in a newsletter. Accessing well-chosen Web sites beats paying for specialty software!

RESOURCES

Keeping Bookmarks Online

What is more frustrating than book-marking a great Web site at home and not having access to it at school, or vice versa? In the past at Lenski, each time a teacher found a good Web site to use in a unit of study, someone had to go to each computer individually to bookmark the site prior to student use, or students had to type in the URLs at their computers. With 300 computers in the building, the task of book-marking any site took hours.

Three years ago, Lenski started keeping bookmarks on a free Web bookmark manager, www.ikeepbookmarks.com and set this site as the browser's home page on all the computers in the building. This simplifies directing students to Web sites and makes it easier to update the list of Web sites. When we are at conferences, we can easily add Web sites that we learn about or show sites to people we meet. Registration on the site is easy and the "Add to Bookmarks" pop-up for adding Web sites to the list makes management painless. Although www.ikeepbookmarks.com offers a free service, schools can also subscribe to the site for faster response times.

The disadvantage of keeping bookmarks on a Web site is the possibility that the Web site will be down for service just when you need the site most. The iKeepBookmarks.com site is rarely down, but twice during early morning staff development, I couldn't get to the site. For that reason, I believe it is wise to have a back-up bookmark manager.

The following bookmark manager sites are all free. Each has a distinct look and feel and any would work well in a school.

Portaportal (www.portaportal.com): This bookmark storage site has an uncluttered appearance, despite the advertising along the side of the account pages. Portaportal provides an excellent tutorial that explains all the symbols on each page and how to manage an account. Guests can access an account as long as they know the account login name; no password is required. The site managers have made creating an account and adding bookmarks easy. There is even a link to a sample page so that a teacher can see the look and feel of a bookmark account before registering.

Sitejot (www.sitejot.com): Sitejot's interface is very simple without a lot of text. Accounts can be public (open to view by anyone) or private (protected with a password). On the same page for adding a site or a category is a button for importing a list of Web sites from another location. Sitejot says it is advertisement-free, but this refers to banner and pop-up ads. There are a few ads at the top and side of the pages.

Mylinkvault (www.mylinkvault.com): The storage folders on MyLinkVault can be color-coded by grade level, an advantage with young non-readers. Editing and adding Web sites, as well as expanding and collapsing the folders, are easy through two buttons on each folder. The demo at this site allows guests to try out all the functions of adding and deleting links and categories, changing folder colors, expanding and collapsing folders, and locking and unlocking the editing. Accounts can be made public or private. The site has advertising at the bottom of each page.

Continued

myHq (www.myhq.com): The registration page for myHq looks busy and very text-heavy. So do the other information pages, but this site offers a lot. Bookmarks can be imported to or exported from myHq easily. Registrants have total control over the look and feel of their pages and the site is free of banner ads. One advantage to this site is the ability to "grab" bookmarks from other accounts on the site. If several people are sharing links, and one person updates a link, the links update for everyone. Needing to log onto the site each time would make it difficult to use in some schools. This is the only bookmark manager that mentions supporting the Opera Web browser.

MyBookmarks (www.mybookmarks.com): Another free service, MyBookmarks uses a very simple layout and design to make loading pages fast. New accounts can import bookmarks from their Web browsers. This site has a minimum of instruction.

FIGURE 12.4 MyBookmarks has a pleasing background and manages folders similar to www.ikeepbookmarks.com. For students accustomed to using folders, this lay-out works well.

GlobusPort (www.globusport.com): GlobusPort is sponsored by EK, Inc., a technology company. Their free Web page for organizing bookmarks has simple tools and a good help section. Their links look similar to some search engine home pages. Organizing Web sites within a category is very easy, so a teacher could put the most commonly used Web sites at the top. Site users are required to login, so this might not be viable for some schools.

The Internet introduces issues that schools have not had to address in the past. When students were limited to library books for research, teachers knew that the resources had already been reviewed by professionals, so students could generally trust their resources. A librarian could teach a few lessons on library organization and proper citation prior to a research project, and release students to work semi-independently. As students gain experience with the Internet, though, teachers need to recognize that even elementary students now need skills in efficient and effective searching, evaluating sources for bias and authority, and ethics.

At one time, schools talked about library literacy and technology literacy as though they were separate skill sets. Now schools need to address information literacy—the variety of skills that students need to be safe and successful in using technology as one tool of research. One excellent source for a list of information literacy skills, complete with lesson plans and the appropriate grade level for introducing each skill is the 21st Century Literacies home page (www.kn.att.com/wired/21stcent/gradelevel.html; see Information Literacy Resources sidebar), which addresses 21st-century learning.

Many sites address Internet safety, some more effectively than others. Currently, two sites provide complementary resources for teaching safety, Cyber Smart! and NetSmartz Workshop.

Cyber Smart! (www.cybersmartcurriculum.org) offers a "free K–8 curriculum empowering students to use the Internet safely, responsibly and effectively." A PDF file under More Free Stuff shows how the lessons are aligned to ISTE's NETS for Students. The organization maintains that the curriculum will always be free for public use.

NetSmartz Workshop (www.netsmartz.org) has separate sections for kids, teens, teachers, and parents, each with appropriate information. This site does a good job of addressing cyber bullying through video clips and worksheets. A teacher could easily project the video clips for whole class viewing prior to a discussion.

FIGURE 12.5 The lively look and feel of the Kids Page in Net Smartz will engage elementary students while they learn about cyber safety.

E-MAIL (3–5)

E-mail has potential to be a valuable resource for collaborative learning. Some schools configure their e-mail services to allow students to e-mail only people within their school or district. Others participate in global student e-mail services where student communications are limited to other students, but these may be anywhere in the world. Some schools let students use free e-mail services offered on the Web to anyone. In any of these cases, teachers need to monitor student communications in order to prevent inappropriate messages. In our experience, some intermediate students lack the maturity to communicate with other students without resorting to name calling, criticizing, or revealing personal information.

Ideally, students using e-mail should be communicating with students in another school where the two teachers have agreed to specific purposes for the communication. However, this style of communication requires that all students have sufficient time and access to computers to compose and send timely responses, a challenge in any classroom.

Purposes for e-mail correspondence should support curricular learning, which might simply include authentic reasons for writing. Overall, though, students have more to write when they have common purposes such as science and social studies units. First-grade students at Lenski research mammals and visit the Denver zoo. How interesting it would be for them to correspond with students in Australia or Africa about mammals that live there. I remember thinking that koalas must be soft and cuddly until an Australian friend, who had been to an Australian petting zoo, said the koala's fur is actually coarse and bristly. Students can't always get such information from a book!

When fourth-grade students work on U.S. state reports, they often e-mail questions to state tourism boards, but they would truly enjoy gathering that information through e-mail relationships with students in those states. They would then get kid perspectives on the states' schools, recreation, tourism, and famous citizens.

Teachers who have visited other countries have set up classroom exchanges of information about schools or culture. Creating reading groups that span two classrooms, whether through the district intranet or through an Internet connection outside the district, can generate intriguing discussions, either through e-mail or blogging.

One teacher uses internal e-mail to have her second-grade reading group discuss their book. Students love reading responses from others in the group. Another teacher uses intranet e-mail to have partners dialogue among themselves and with her about what they are learning, wondering about, and predicting.

If students will be reading a book set in another country, they could create e-mail discussion groups with students in that country. The students who live there can respond to questions about how the culture is reflected in the books. If, at the same time, some of those students are reading books set near the first students' homes, the process can work in reverse.

E-mail exchanges do not have to include the entire class. In some cases, a teacher may choose, because of students' maturity levels or sense of engagement, to limit an e-mail correspondence to only a few students in the class. An example would be to use e-mail between groups of high achievers or to have one student represent the class as the class secretary. This eliminates the need for constant access to computers for the whole class.

E-mail has also been an effective way for students to write to their teachers about issues that are troubling them.

Blogging (3–5)

A web log, or blog, is another tool that can be used for educational purposes. A fairly recent phenomenon, blogging provides better opportunities for groups of students to communicate than e-mail. Teachers have options for where they will post blogs.

Many blogging programs on the Internet are free and easy to design. Teachers can opt to keep the areas private so that only those invited to join can post a new thread. Currently, private sites also remain invisible to search engines so that outsiders are not tempted to join. When using an Internet-hosted blog, teachers might consider having new posts first submitted via e-mail to the teacher (moderator). That way, if students write inappropriate entries, teachers can block the entries from the site.

Some districts host blogs on their local servers. Depending on the configuration, these blogs may be available only through the intranet (internally in the district) or through any Internet-connected computer. Districts that host distance-learning platforms can use the same platforms for blogs.

Whether blogs are feasible for schools may depend on students' home and school access to computers, ITS's policies concerning the hosting of blogs, and the level of public relations done to prepare the parent community. Like e-mail, blogging requires that students have ready access to computers. If students do not have Internet-connected computers at home, then teachers need to provide time and access during the school day. Some schools allow students to use computers in libraries during literacy times.

The attitude of ITS toward blogging will impact whether the district hosts a blog on the local server or teachers need to find online hosting. As with any online service, teachers should pay attention to whether students will encounter advertising or strangers on the site.

Not all parents are comfortable with the concept of blogging, so in many communities, it will be necessary to assure parents that the site will be safe and monitored. One possible way to win parents over is to host a grade-level or class blog for them. They can use blogs to talk to teachers and other parents in a private environment, which is the benefit to them, and teachers can demonstrate that blogging can be a protected environment for students.

RESOURCES

Free Blogging Resouces

Teachers can, and should, try out blogging before introducing it to students. At these free blogging and hosting sites, teachers can create accounts and invite some family members or friends to join a discussion. Keeping the blog private, at least at first, will limit the participants to only those invited to join. At the elementary school level, if the blog is hosted on an outside server, keeping the blog private will provide the strongest protection for students. The following are only a few examples of the many free blogging services on the Internet.

Blogger (www.blogger.com): One of the most popular, easy to use, and commonly known blog account sites, Blogger is now owned by Google. Once you have created your blog, you can determine whether to host the blog on your own server or with Google. This site will continue to be upgraded and to offer more services.

LiveJournal (www.livejournal.com): Built on open source software, LiveJournal offers free diary or blogging space. Free accounts have access to many account features and are certainly sufficient for casual bloggers, but subscribers do receive more services. Teachers can keep their accounts private, so students encounter only their peers. The site is funded through subscribers, so it does not have advertising.

Multiply (http://multiply.com): Multiply supports social networking services beyond just blogging. Not only does it supply unlimited storage space for pictures, videos, music, and blogs, it offers a live discussion and, at the user's option, notifies his or her social network when the person makes any changes to the site. Account owners can keep their blogs private for people they invite to join them. Multiply offers a paid service as well with additional features. On a tour of the site, I noticed that each service on the site has the same window for doing the work. The window for writing blogs looks like an e-mail page.

Parents and some administrators question the academic value of blogging. A Lenski fifth-grade teacher used blogging to continue classroom discussions on a novel students were reading. By requiring all students to participate and to post meaningful discussion, she guaranteed that all students would be heard. In every class, teachers have students who stay in the background and others who dominate any conversation. Blogging evens out the contributions, particularly if everyone is required to participate. Often blogging reveals ideas and opinions that would have been unspoken in the classroom.

Personal File Storage (4–5)

Teachers regularly face challenges when students want to transport files between home and school. While some schools require flash drives as part of the school supply list, at Lenski, the need for transporting files is not high enough to make it a requirement. Generally, Lenski students work on projects at school so that they don't fall into the practice of depending on a parent to perfect it.

RESOURCES

NiceNet—More Than Just a Storage Locker

Of the many resources Lenski teachers tried for online storage lockers, NiceNet (www.nicenet.org) has emerged as the favorite. But NiceNet is much more than an online storage locker—it's a mini-version of a distance-learning tool. Provided as a free service, NiceNet allows teachers to create classes and give students an access code so that they can enroll themselves. Students can upload files and communicate with one another, and all information is visible to the teacher. Tools include conferencing, document sharing, scheduling, personal messaging, and link sharing. Teachers can create assignments and students can submit them within the tool.

If students use NiceNet as a way to upload files so that they can access them from home or school, make certain that they occasionally clean house. Otherwise the list of shared documents can grow overwhelming. Creating naming conventions would also help keep the files organized.

Consider this tool for collaborative work. A teacher could create a separate class for each collaborative group and monitor the group's work easily from any Web-connected computer.

However, in some classes on some projects, students need to transport their files back and forth. Lenski has experimented with online personal file storage sites. Online file storage services are free password-protected briefcases or lockers where students can upload files and access them again from any Internet-connected computer. Many free e-mail services on the Web also provide online storage lockers.

Web Design (3–5)

Some schools teach Web design to intermediate students. Teachers who opt for this instruction need to be careful to protect students' privacy and to observe copyright laws. District policies concerning photos and names of students on the Web vary greatly. Find out your district's expectations before you encourage students to publish their work on the Web. Also, be certain that students don't incorporate copyrighted material, such as downloaded pictures, into their projects and then post them on the Internet.

Video (4–5)

Videotaping and computer-based video editing will be most successful with small groups of students, such as summer workshops or gifted/talented pull-out programs. Additionally, video editing requires user-friendly software and large amounts of computer memory. Some schools find it an excellent tool for hooking the visual and experiential learners. After a marginally successful experience with video under a grant, Lenski teachers shied away from using it again. Recently, access to more powerful computers and user-friendly editing software has renewed teachers' interest.

Based on the lessons learned from the first unsuccessful attempt to use video, teachers will start with small projects to let students learn a few skills at a time. At first, teachers want to have students simply insert more video into slide shows. Some students have successfully inserted videos in the past, but generally it has been without teacher assistance. Now, all intermediate students will learn how to embed video clips into slide shows.

Lenski has access to video clips through Discovery Education's *unitedstreaming* as of 2006–07, so students and teachers began with clips downloaded from that service. Additionally, students can access NASA's video collections during the space exploration unit.

When students have learned how to integrate video into slide shows, then they will learn about editing clips. Using editable clips from Discovery Education's *unitedstreaming* will give students content-based video to combine with still pictures, voice-overs, and music in short productions. I foresee some students choosing this option rather than a brochure to get across messages about the dangers of smoking and drug and alcohol abuse. These could be developed as 30-second public service announcements.

Eventually, teachers would like students to shoot and edit videos at school. These could be public service announcements about playground rules, bad weather safety, or lunchroom conduct expectations. Students might also create enactments of historic periods, clips about a topic they've researched, or highlights of a class event. Dictionary Day videos that include clips of students explaining their words, text with the words and meanings, and music would help students retain the vocabulary even better.

Freeware

Finding educational freeware has become more difficult as Internet sites have proliferated. That's because the freeware either has turned into interactive Web activities or has become commercial. However, some freeware offers excellent opportunities for students to practice key skills, such as geography, letter recognition, phonemic awareness, and telling time. In addition to the freeware presented in chapter 4, the open-source community places many free programs on the Web.

One excellent free program is E-toys, which is programmed in Squeak. Based on the same philosophy as Logo, this software encourages students to discover science and math concepts through simple programming. Squeak is not intuitive, so a student will need models to follow in order to learn the potential of the software. Fortunately, the Web site www.squeakland.org has adequate samples and instructions to help students begin exploration.

FIGURE 12.6 Squeak, an open-ended software for programming, encourages exploration and learning, as advocated by Dr. Seymour Papert. Students can create drawings and then animate them to explore math, science, and programming concepts. Squeak is complex, so students need guidance to learn how the program works at the beginning. Since Squeak is free, students can download it at home as well and attempt to recreate projects shown on the Web site.

Digital Cameras

As the price of digital cameras has dropped, their popularity has soared. Where once only teachers used the cameras, now Lenski provides a set of eight durable, inexpensive digital cameras (under $20 each) for student use. When classes go on field trips, several students act as class photographers and record what they consider important. These pictures are then loaded on the server for class use when students write about the field trip. Interestingly, one noticeable difference between pictures taken by teachers and by students has been the subject matter. In our experience, teachers take action shots of students involved in activities, while students take pictures of their new learnings. For example, on a trip to an historical park, the teachers photographed students cooking fritters and panning for gold, while students photographed close-ups of the fritters and gold panning tools. Students as young as second grade have managed the digital cameras on field trips.

The discovery that students fill shapes with photos as background has changed how teachers view the digital photos. Often teachers would limit the students to one or two pictures on a field trip report, even though students had access to 30-50 photos. Now teachers are thinking about how students can use a collage of photos to convey a theme or can create a photo album page of one aspect of a unit. With student digital cameras, student groups can collaborate on creating A-B-C or 1-2-3 books on shapes, colors, seasons, or other themes to give to their buddy classes.

Because of shortages of time and money, no school can embrace every new technology that shows promise. Annually, Lenski teachers explore areas where they can expand their skills. This may be the use of tools, such as digital microscopes or personal digital assistants, or expansion of a project idea, such as giving students more autonomy

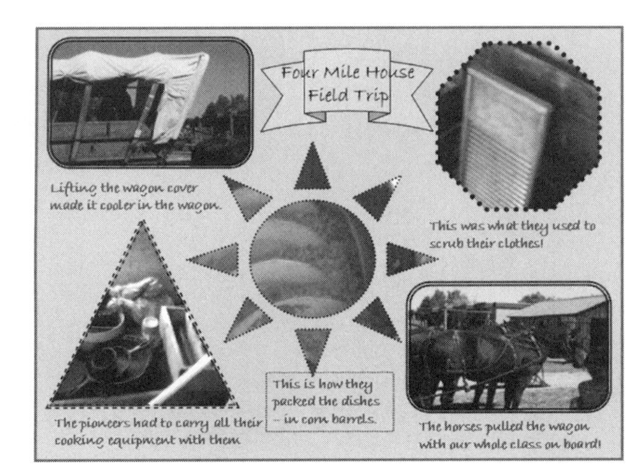

FIGURE 12.7 This photo album page uses students' digital pictures from a field trip to Four Mile House in the Denver Metro area. During the field trip, students learned about pioneers, the Plains Indians, and gold panning. When I first saw the students' pictures, I assumed the middle photo was a mistake and suggested that the teacher delete it. The student photographer explained that it was her best picture because it showed how the pioneers packed their china so it wouldn't break.

with their slideshows or increasing the scope of visual vocabulary lessons. We look longingly at schools with 1:1 laptops initiatives, video conferencing capability, and funding designated for technology. We cannot do everything we want, but we can, and do, continue to grow, explore, risk, and learn in order to help students achieve their best.

Conclusion

Putting It Together

CHANGING ANY CULTURE REQUIRES PIONEERS TO TAKE RISKS, overcome resistance, and endure criticism. As Lenski continues to blaze a trail in the district by implementing a strong collaborative model and infusing technology into all aspects of teaching and learning, the staff recognizes that it would be easier to maintain the status quo. The school already has high test scores, involved parents, and full enrollment because of 50% choice. Parents express high satisfaction with the educational opportunities their children receive.

Even though maintaining the status quo would be easier, moving forward by improving instructional practices promotes Lenski's core value: doing what's best for kids. Using technology regularly to engage students in high-quality learning experiences motivates students to actively participate in the learning process. It's fascinating that, in my experiences at Lenski, students who use technology daily in the classroom often think of learning as easy and fun, even though they work very hard. When I evaluate test results, many of these students accomplish more than a year's growth during the school year.

The challenge of elementary schools is to prepare students for a world that is beyond the teachers' imaginations. Considering how quickly technology has evolved from clumsy calculators to today's marvels, it's likely that kindergarten children will be using technology in new and amazing ways by the middle school years. Trying to prepare them for that future requires disconnecting from the belief that students need to learn specific skills and focusing instead on teaching them the core skills that will enable them to adapt as technology changes.

Students must learn to locate, evaluate, and apply information to make nimble decisions, solve problems, and think creatively. They need to develop strong ethical values and a sense of personal responsibility for decisions. Their fast-changing world will require flexibility, self-motivation, and efficiency.

The use of technology in elementary school can help students build many of the core skills while it gives them proficiency with evolving technologies. Rather than thinking of technology skills as an end, teachers need to recognize that the technical skills simply provide the means for increasing students' efficiency and effectiveness in expressing what they know.

The collaborative model that Lenski has adopted, where everyone shares the responsibility for students' success, continues to evolve into a stronger network every year. Collaboration increases the staff's collective strength. Teachers have support for refining lesson plans, helping struggling students, motivating dawdlers, or just presenting key concepts in different ways. Support teachers and teaching assistants play important roles in students' progress, and this motivates the support staff to take the initiative when they see needs that they can help to meet. Overall, the staff strives to improve instructional practices to focus on what students learn versus what teachers teach.

The infusion of technology into the daily business of teaching and learning changes how we behave. Teachers let technology tools handle administrative tasks so that they can focus on individualizing instruction for students. Students embrace technologies as tools for discovering the answers to their questions and demonstrating what they know. Parent-teacher communications are transitioning to electronic means, which saves time. Best of all, teachers have learned to harness the power of technology to improve students' recall of content area learning. So often, very simple uses of technology, such as visual vocabulary, have long-lasting effects.

The role of technology teachers at Lenski has been facilitator, mentor, and procurer. Trecie and I can give teachers the tools and ideas to facilitate the use of technology, but we can't integrate technology into their daily classroom practices. We can model and encourage high-quality instruction, but we can't force teachers to change their instructional strategies. We can pursue grants, donations, and other outside funding to procure equipment, but we can't make anyone use that equipment to improve instruction. We are conduits, not the electricity that lights up students' minds. Lenski classroom teachers get the credit for using technology to improve student learning.

Throughout this book, I've shared my best thinking about the transforming power of technology when it is used appropriately at the elementary level. Over six years, some of the central lessons we've learned at Lenski can be summed in this way:

1. **No one can succeed alone.** By myself, I cannot change even one classroom. But with a shared vision and commitment to do what is best for kids, the teachers and school leaders, including me, can change students' experiences in our school. Barb DeSpain, the principal, has created a culture of collaboration that fosters instructional risk-taking for the sake of kids.

   We take those risks together because we believe, based on research and experience, that those risks will result in better student achievement. The infusion of technology started as a risk, because it pushed teachers to let students use tools that the teachers considered difficult to use and manage. Six years later, teachers cannot imagine teaching any other way, and students' portfolios serve as concrete evidence of students' high levels of achievement.
2. **Technology provides a means for engaging students in the important business of learning to learn.** Technology tools entice some students into the learning process, but the tools themselves or the skills to use the tools cannot be the focus of instruction. Students learn to use a hammer; they don't learn hammers. The same is true for technology. Students become skilled at knowing when and how to use technology tools to support and demonstrate their learning, but learning is the goal.
3. **Being on the cutting edge isn't as important as being farther along than you were last year.** Some people will seize the newest gadgets and look for ways to make them relevant for education. I'm thankful for them because often their experiences clarify for me what is truly a gadget and what is a useful tool. But being on the cutting edge of a tool with little instructional value is not as valuable for students as regularly and thoughtfully introducing new tools and ideas that support curricular targets.
4. **Every child deserves daily access to technology tools for purposeful learning.** Some students have minute-by-minute access, so even when teachers provide daily access, the gap in technology experiences widens. But just using a computer or projector or portable word processor each day is not enough. The use of technology must lead to meaningful learning. No teacher has sufficient time to teach students everything in the standards. Wasting instructional time with purposeless technology, even if that time is part of the specials rotation, is irresponsible. Playing games that don't support curricular learning or drilling on skills students have already mastered robs students of instructional opportunity.

Teachers cannot teach with 20th-century methods and produce 21st-century citizens. Schools must blend collaborative learning, effective instructional practices, and the ubiquitous use of technology for both students and staff if they truly desire to train students for their futures.

Sources

Kulik, J. A. (2003, May). *Effects of instructional technology in elementary and secondary schools: What controlled evaluation studies say*. Retrieved June 25, 2006, from www.cddre.org/Resources/KulikEffectsofITinElandSecSchools.pdf

Marzano, R. J., Pickering, D. J., & Pollock, J. E. (2001). Classroom instruction that works: Research-based strategies for increasing student achievement. Alexandria, VA: Association for Supervision and Curriculum Development.

Stratham, D. S., & Torell, C. R. (1996). *Computers in the classroom: The impact of technology on student learning*. Retrieved June 25, 2006, from www.temple.edu/lss/htmlpublications/spotlights/200/spot206.htm

Figure and Illustration Credits

Fig. 4.1: © Computers for Schools Association. Reprinted with permission.
Fig. 4.2: © AlphaSmart Direct, Inc. Reprinted with permission.
Fig. 4.3: © QuickPAD Technology Corporation. Reprinted with permission.
Page 75; Fig. 6.2: Created by Lindsey Y.
Fig. 6.3: Created by Ally P.
Fig. 6.4: Created by Trevor Y.
Fig. 6.5: Created by Kelsey V.
Fig. 6.6: Created by Andrew C.
Fig. 6.7: Created by Jake P. and Sam M.
Fig. 6.8: Created by Maria K.
Fig. 6.9: Created by Kristin C.
Fig. 6.10: Created by Jason B., Pierce M., Zach C., and Peter H.
Fig. 6.13: © 2001 Southwest Educational Development Corporation and Southwest Educational Development Laboratory. All rights reserved. Reprinted with permission.
Fig. 6.14: © Sesame Workshop.
Page 89: Created by Drew W.
Fig. 7.1: © Utah State Office of Education (USOE). Reprinted with permission.
Fig. 7.3: Created by Natalie S.
Fig. 7.4: Created by Hannah B.
Fig. 7.5: Created by Graham M. and Andrew T.
Fig. 7.6: Created by Dylan C. and Connor S.
Fig. 7.7: Created by Krista G. and Kelly M.
Fig. 7.8: Created by Cece D.
Fig. 8.1: Created by Emma C.
Fig. 8.2: © Writing Fix. Reprinted with permission.
Fig. 8.3: © Answers Corporation. Reprinted with permission.
Fig. 9.1: Created by Tess G.
Fig. 9.2: Created by Samantha W., Mitch G., Adam Q., Summer S., and Haley M.
Page 115; Fig. 9.3: Created by Natalie C.
Fig. 9.5: Reprinted with permission of www.planetozkids.com.
Fig. 9.6: Created by Karyn H.
Page 125: Created by Ben L.
Fig. 10.1: Created by Ally P.
Fig. 10.2: Created by Hiatt T.
Fig. 10.3: Created by Elli S. and Zac G.
Fig. 10.6: Created by Allison B.
Fig. 10.7: Created by Carli M.
Fig. 10.8: Created by Ty S.
Fig. 10.9: Created by Evelyn H.
Fig. 10.10: Created by Kelly M.
Fig. 10.12: Created by Megan B.
Fig. 10.13: Created by Nate K.
Fig. 11.1: Created by Dallin J.
Fig. 11.2: Created by Meghan G.
Page 145; Fig. 11.3: Created by Courtney W.
Fig. 12.1: © 2006 Starfall Website. Reprinted with permission.
Fig. 12.2: Reprinted with permission of Rick Meyers, creator of Zoopz.
Fig. 12.3: Reprinted with permission of ReadWriteThink (www.readwritethink.org), a nonprofit MarcoPolo Web site maintained by the International Reading Association (IRA) and the National Council of Teachers of English (NCTE), with support from the Verizon Foundation.
Fig. 12.4: © MyBookmarks.com, LLC. Reprinted with permission.
Fig. 12.5: © National Center for Missing & Exploited Children and Boys & Girls Club of America. Reprinted with permission.
Fig. 12.6: Reprinted with permission from Viewpoints Research Institute, Inc., Glendale, California.

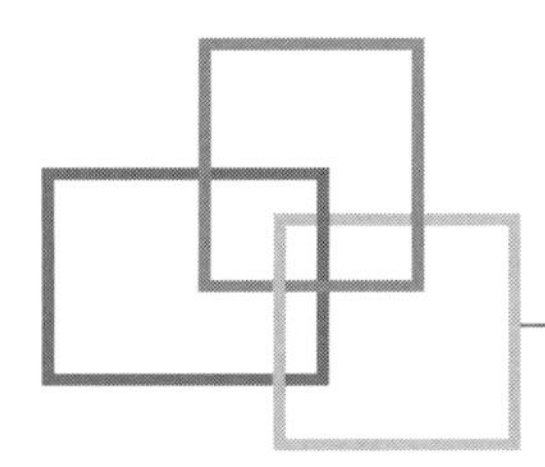

Appendix A

Managing the Classroom with One Computer

MANY LAB TEACHERS HAVE ENOUGH COMPUTERS so that all the students work simultaneously on projects. This is a far different proposition from the classroom where a teacher may have only one computer and thirty students.

What can you realistically do if your classroom has one or two computers? The answer depends, to a large extent, on your teaching style. Some teachers (and some age levels) need clearly defined procedures and schedules. Others allow students to have a lot of autonomy. Still other classroom teachers reserve computer use for select purposes or students.

Whatever your plan, consider carefully how you set up the computer area. If students will be using the Internet, the monitor should be easily viewed from your location so that if a child ends up on an inappropriate site, you can intervene. A basket with pencils and scratch paper will allow students to jot notes. A portable file case with a file for each child will make it easy for students to store worksheets over several days. If children have a specific length of time for a task at the computer, place a timer nearby so that they know when their time is up. Be certain that students have headphones; even if the computer activity doesn't have sound, the headphones cancel out classroom noise.

As you read the following ideas, look for those that match your situation and teaching style. Remember no one idea is better than another. The best idea is the one that works for you.

Computers as Activity Centers

Teachers can use the computer as an activity center for one or more students at a time. This is particularly appropriate for Web sites, although, as indicated below, teachers can provide templates for students to do projects as well.

During a study of animals, a pair of students sharing a computer and using two sets of headphones can visit a zoo Web site or a digital photo collection to take notes about the animals they see. This type of pairing, particularly of students of unequal skill levels, promotes collaboration and allows one student to model skills for another. If needed, teacher-created worksheets can guide students through a Web site or a specialty program.

For primary students, Web sites and specialty software also offer excellent practice in basic reading and math skills. Teachers can use these tools to target specific skills to reinforce the day's reading or math lesson.

If primary teachers want to use the computers for project activities as well, a little advance work will set students up for success. The teacher creates a master folder of templates for the projects students may work on during the year. Suggested teacher-designed templates would be drawing pages divided into two, three, four, and five sections; framed paragraphs for reporting on a research project; pre-designed slide shows with text boxes where students can click and add text; assessment slides for specific skills such as coin recognition or word-picture matching; and others. I recommend more templates than a teacher expects to get to in the year. The goal is to create one master folder that will cover most projects students will attempt during the year. That will cut down on the number of times a teacher needs to create new templates and copy them to all the folders.

When the master folder is finished, save a copy to a server account, if possible, or on a flash drive. Then copy the master folder on the desktop and paste as many duplicate folders as there are students in the class. Rename each folder with the name of student in the class. During the year, students can open their folders and choose the projects they've been asked to do. When they've finished, if they save and close the file, their work will go back into the same folders, so there's no danger of losing their work. Teachers can decide whether students should print their work or whether the teacher would rather proofread prior to printing. Parents or high school volunteers can help manage the proofing and printing.

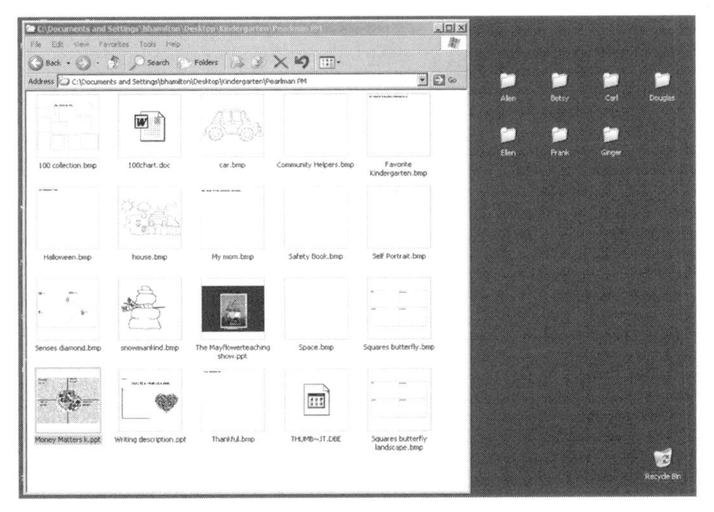

FIGURE A.1 This screenshot of a computer desktop illustrates one way to simplify the use of technology in the primary classroom where students may not be capable of accessing a server. The white window on the left shows the sample contents of a master folder of templates for a year's projects. Copies of that master folder have been pasted in the blue area on the right and renamed with the names of students in the class. During the year, as the class prepares to start a project contained in the folders, students can open their own folders, find the correct project name, and do the work. When they save and close their work, the projects will be saved in their folders.

Computers for Specific Students

In some classrooms during specific times of the day, teachers reserve the computers for students who need intervention or separation from others. For instance, children with poor motor skills but reasonable typing ability may be more successful if their written work is completed on a computer or portable word processor rather than longhand. A teacher may even use voice recognition software so that children with limited keyboarding skills can still record their thoughts as rough drafts. This strategic use of computers should not deny access to the remaining students, who should have their own targeted time on the computers. However, it is one way a teacher can differentiate for students with high needs.

In one case, I saw a primary teacher use computers as a management tool for three students who regularly disrupted reading centers. These students worked on targeted individual projects during their reading center time. Later in the day, the remaining students in the class had computer and activity center times while the three students were pulled out by a specialist for reading instruction.

Reward Time

When students complete their work early, giving them reward time on the computer sometimes motivates less productive classmates to work faster and more steadily. Some teachers even let students spend reward time on the computer before or after school. This is particularly motivating to students who don't have Internet access or a computer at home. Generally, teachers should have specific purposes for the reward time—indiscriminate Internet hopping can lead to problems. Placing a folder of shortcuts to educational freeware programs or other software owned by the school can reward students but still supplement classroom instruction.

Work Completion Time

When students do not complete their technology-based products on schedule, some teachers ask them to sign up for work completion time on the computers. During free-choice time in the classroom, students rotate on the computers according to the order in which they are signed up. Sometimes students miss recess or spend time before or after school on the computers to catch up on their work. At Lenski, we avoid sending computer-based projects home for completion when students have been dawdling because we've learned that many parents will complete the work for them rather than hold the children responsible.

Asking students to give up choice time, or even running an occasional Saturday school, is much more effective for teaching responsibility. Some schools even work out a way to have parents or teacher assistants provide before- or after-school study hall time in a computer lab for work completion. Teachers assign study hall in the same way that high schools assign detention. The students get individual attention if they need it, and the teachers do not give up their personal time. Providing additional time for some students to become more proficient with technology literacy can be compared to providing supplemental support for reading, writing, and math literacies.

Rotating Schedules

In some classrooms students get computer access on a rotating schedule. Students have several choices of activities, such as keyboarding practice, math fact drill, project completion, or original artwork. Computer time is limited to a quarter or half an hour at a time, and students take responsibility for handing over the computer to the next person on the list. Since the list rotates, all students get equal time without teacher intervention.

Computers on an As-Needed Basis

In some schools or at some grade levels, teachers agree that any unused computer is available for anyone else. So, when teachers have a handful of students needing to complete work and only one computer in the classroom, they send the remaining to neighboring classrooms and, if those computers are free, the students work quietly there. Students understand that if they misbehave in any way, particularly if they disrupt the classroom they're visiting, they will lose the privilege of going to another classroom and will need to complete their work during recess time.

Mini-labs

In some schools, teachers contribute their single computers to a mini-lab in an alcove or hallway near the classrooms. This can be particularly effective if several classrooms feed into a common area. That way, no one gives up precious space in a classroom, and everyone has access to more than one computer at a time. A whiteboard schedule allows teachers to reserve the computers for specific days or times. A parent volunteer can supervise students. Teachers can set the expectation that if any children are unruly or unproductive in the mini-lab, they lose the privilege of working outside the classroom. This means they will probably need to make other arrangements for work completion, such as losing recess or, on rare occasions, attending Saturday school.

Quasi-computer Center

Simple, inexpensive word processors (See chapter 2) cost far less than computers and can be used to supplement the computer center. While the classroom computer is being used as an activity center for a reading activity, the word processor can be used for writing practice. Perhaps each student starts by typing his/her name, and then writes a poem, a response to a prompt, or the answer to a question about a book. Later in the day, the teacher or a volunteer downloads all the text to a computer, adds formatting and/or proofreads, and prints the text for the teacher to share with the class.

These word processors can even go home for students to write on their own time. In the morning, the students download their evening's work and save it for later touch-up.

Projection Unit

With a projection unit, a teacher can turn any computer into a large or small group learning center. Teachers can access interactive Web sites and demonstrate their use. Then in small groups, students can take turns using the mouse to activate the Web site.

Teachers or students can use the projector to demonstrate a technology skill to be used later in a lab setting or at classroom computers. Students can also use the projector to show their completed work.

Students can even collaboratively search an online database for information about a curricular topic of study. Together they can take notes or extend the search to related topics. To enhance such collaboration further, have one or more children record the notes on a portable word processor for the entire group.

Some schools teach all technology skills as a large group experience. Students take turns managing the mouse, or a teacher uses a wireless tablet or presenter mouse to control the computer from anywhere in the room. While using this model exclusively does not give students sufficient experience with technology to become proficient, it does provide computer experience in a technology-poor environment.

The drawback of a one-computer classroom is the difficulty of infusing technology into daily work. Every project takes longer when students have to wait for their turns, and teachers typically need to simplify the projects so that students can complete them quickly. Out of necessity, some students will be working on a unit project long after the unit is done, unless the teacher differentiates by having one group of students work on one unit and the next group do a project related to the second unit, etc.

However, teachers cannot stop using computers just because of a scarcity of equipment. All students need quality experiences with technology; so all teachers bear the responsibility to make the best use of the equipment they get. Ideally, in a year, students have opportunities to produce quality products, visit interactive Web sites, and work collaboratively with peers on content-driven, technology-based projects.

Every year, teachers should attempt at least one new idea that takes them out of their comfort zones and allows students to experiment with tools or applications. The problems that arise when teachers try new applications or projects can be looked on as learning and problem-solving opportunities—for the students!

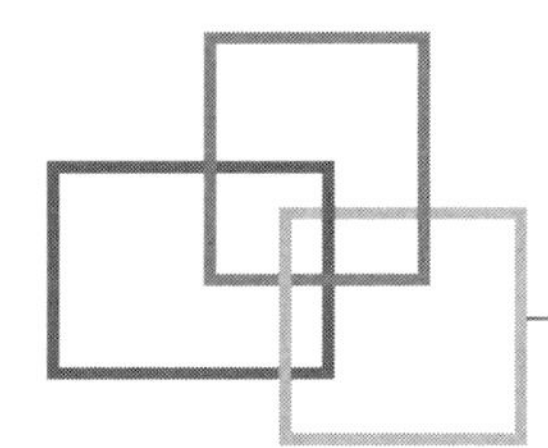

Appendix B

National Educational Technology Standards

National Educational Technology Standards for Students (NETS•S)

The National Educational Technology Standards for students are divided into six broad categories. Standards within each category are to be introduced, reinforced, and mastered by students. Teachers can use these standards as guidelines for planning technology-based activities in which students achieve success in learning, communication, and life skills.

1. Basic Operations and Concepts

- Students demonstrate a sound understanding of the nature and operation of technology systems.
- Students are proficient in the use of technology.

2. Social, Ethical, and Human issues

- Students understand the ethical, cultural, and societal issues related to technology.
- Students practice responsible use of technology systems, information, and software.
- Students develop positive attitudes toward technology uses that support lifelong learning, collaboration, personal pursuits, and productivity.

3. Technology Productivity Tools

- Students use technology tools to enhance learning, increase productivity, and promote creativity.
- Students use productivity tools to collaborate in constructing technology-enhanced models, preparing publications, and producing other creative works.

4. Technology Communications Tools

- Students use telecommunications to collaborate, publish, and interact with peers, experts, and other audiences.
- Students use a variety of media and formats to communicate information and ideas effectively to multiple audiences.

5. Technology Research Tools

- Students use technology to locate, evaluate, and collect information from a variety of sources.
- Students use technology tools to process data and report results.
- Students evaluate and select new information resources and technological innovations based on the appropriateness to specific tasks.

6. Technology Problem-solving and Decision-making Tools

- Students use technology resources for solving problems and making informed decisions.
- Students employ technology in the development of strategies for solving problems in the real world.

National Educational Technology Standards for Teachers (NETS•T)

All classroom teachers should be prepared to meet the following standards and performance indicators.

I. Technology Operations and Concepts

Teachers demonstrate a sound understanding of technology operations and concepts. Teachers:

A. demonstrate introductory knowledge, skills, and understanding of concepts related to technology (as described in the ISTE National Educational Technology Standards for Students).

B. demonstrate continual growth in technology knowledge and skills to stay abreast of current and emerging technologies.

II. Planning and Designing Learning Environments and Experiences

Teachers plan and design effective learning environments and experiences supported by technology. Teachers:

A. design developmentally appropriate learning opportunities that apply technology-enhanced instructional strategies to support the diverse needs of learners.

- **B.** apply current research on teaching and learning with technology when planning learning environments and experiences.
- **C.** identify and locate technology resources and evaluate them for accuracy and suitability.
- **D.** plan for the management of technology resources within the context of learning activities.
- **E.** plan strategies to manage student learning in a technology-enhanced environment.

III. Teaching, Learning, and the Curriculum

Teachers implement curriculum plans that include methods and strategies for applying technology to maximize student learning. Teachers:

- **A.** facilitate technology-enhanced experiences that address content standards and student technology standards.
- **B.** use technology to support learner-centered strategies that address the diverse needs of students.
- **C.** apply technology to develop students' higher-order skills and creativity.
- **D.** manage student learning activities in a technology-enhanced environment.

IV. Assessment and Evaluation

Teachers apply technology to facilitate a variety of effective assessment and evaluation strategies. Teachers:

- **A.** apply technology in assessing student learning of subject matter using a variety of assessment techniques.
- **B.** use technology resources to collect and analyze data, interpret results, and communicate findings to improve instructional practice and maximize student learning.
- **C.** apply multiple methods of evaluation to determine students' appropriate use of technology resources for learning, communication, and productivity.

V. Productivity and Professional Practice

Teachers use technology to enhance their productivity and professional practice. Teachers:

- **A.** use technology resources to engage in ongoing professional development and lifelong learning.
- **B.** continually evaluate and reflect on professional practice to make informed decisions regarding the use of technology in support of student learning.
- **C.** apply technology to increase productivity.
- **D.** use technology to communicate and collaborate with peers, parents, and the larger community in order to nurture student learning.

VI. Social, Ethical, Legal, and Human Issues

Teachers understand the social, ethical, legal, and human issues surrounding the use of technology in PK–12 schools and apply that understanding in practice. Teachers:

A. model and teach legal and ethical practice related to technology use.

B. apply technology resources to enable and empower learners with diverse backgrounds, characteristics, and abilities.

C. identify and use technology resources that affirm diversity.

D. promote safe and healthy use of technology resources.

E. facilitate equitable access to technology resources for all students.

National Educational Technology Standards for Administrators (NETS•A)

All school administrators should be prepared to meet the following standards and performance indicators. These standards are a national consensus among educational stakeholders regarding what best indicates effective school leadership for comprehensive and appropriate use of technology in schools.

I. Leadership and Vision—Educational leaders inspire a shared vision for comprehensive integration of technology and foster an environment and culture conducive to the realization of that vision. Educational leaders:

A. facilitate the shared development by all stakeholders of a vision for technology use and widely communicate that vision.

B. maintain an inclusive and cohesive process to develop, implement, and monitor a dynamic, long-range, and systemic technology plan to achieve the vision.

C. foster and nurture a culture of responsible risk taking and advocate policies promoting continuous innovation with technology.

D. use data in making leadership decisions.

E. advocate for research-based effective practices in use of technology.

F. advocate, on the state and national levels, for policies, programs, and funding opportunities that support implementation of the district technology plan.

II. Learning and Teaching—Educational leaders ensure that curricular design, instructional strategies, and learning environments integrate appropriate technologies to maximize learning and teaching. Educational leaders:

A. identify, use, evaluate, and promote appropriate technologies to enhance and support instruction and standards-based curriculum leading to high levels of student achievement.

B. facilitate and support collaborative technology-enriched learning environments conducive to innovation for improved learning.
C. provide for learner-centered environments that use technology to meet the individual and diverse needs of learners.
D. facilitate the use of technologies to support and enhance instructional methods that develop higher-level thinking, decision-making, and problem-solving skills.
E. provide for and ensure that faculty and staff take advantage of quality professional learning opportunities for improved learning and teaching with technology.

III. Productivity and Professional Practice—Educational leaders apply technology to enhance their professional practice and to increase their own productivity and that of others. Educational leaders:

A. model the routine, intentional, and effective use of technology.
B. employ technology for communication and collaboration among colleagues, staff, parents, students, and the larger community.
C. create and participate in learning communities that stimulate, nurture, and support faculty and staff in using technology for improved productivity.
D. engage in sustained, job-related professional learning using technology resources.
E. maintain awareness of emerging technologies and their potential uses in education.
F. use technology to advance organizational improvement.

IV. Support, Management, and Operations—Educational leaders ensure the integration of technology to support productive systems for learning and administration. Educational leaders:

A. develop, implement, and monitor policies and guidelines to ensure compatibility of technologies.
B. implement and use integrated technology-based management and operations systems.
C. allocate financial and human resources to ensure complete and sustained implementation of the technology plan.
D. integrate strategic plans, technology plans, and other improvement plans and policies to align efforts and leverage resources.
E. implement procedures to drive continuous improvements of technology systems and to support technology-replacement cycles.

V. Assessment and Evaluation—Educational leaders use technology to plan and implement comprehensive systems of effective assessment and evaluation. Educational leaders:

- **A.** use multiple methods to assess and evaluate appropriate uses of technology resources for learning, communication, and productivity.
- **B.** use technology to collect and analyze data, interpret results, and communicate findings to improve instructional practice and student learning.
- **C.** assess staff knowledge, skills, and performance in using technology and use results to facilitate quality professional development and to inform personnel decisions.
- **D.** use technology to assess, evaluate, and manage administrative and operational systems.

VI. Social, Legal, and Ethical Issues—Educational leaders understand the social, legal, and ethical issues related to technology and model responsible decision making related to these issues. Educational leaders:

- **A.** ensure equity of access to technology resources that enable and empower all learners and educators.
- **B.** identify, communicate, model, and enforce social, legal, and ethical practices to promote responsible use of technology.
- **C.** promote and enforce privacy, security, and online safety related to the use of technology.
- **D.** promote and enforce environmentally safe and healthy practices in the use of technology.
- **E.** participate in the development of policies that clearly enforce copyright law and assign ownership of intellectual property developed with district resources.

This material was originally produced as a project of the Technology Standards for School Administrators Collaborative.